Troubled Waters

NEIL DIXON

Troubled
Waters

London EPWORTH PRESS

7162 0327 8

Enquiries should be addressed to
The Methodist Publishing House
Wellington Road
Wimbledon
London SW19 8EU
Printed in Great Britain by
The Garden City Press Limited
Letchworth, Hertfordshire SG6 1JS

Contents

Acknowledgments

The following publishers have kindly given permission for quotations, in excess of one hundred words, from the works named:

Basil Blackwell: Rudolf Schnackenburg, *Baptism in the Thought of St. Paul*

Church Information Office: The report, *Baptism, Thanksgiving and Blessing*

Grove Books: The leaflet, *Thinking about Baptism;* Colin O. Buchanan, *Baptismal Discipline*

Hodder and Stoughton: R. E. O. White, *The Biblical Doctrine of Initiation*

Inter-Varsity Press: Donald Bridge and David Phypers, *The Water that Divides*

SCM Press: The report, *One Lord, One Baptism*

SPCK: Neville Clark and Ronald C.D. Jasper (ed.), *Initiation and Eucharist;* W.F. Flemington, *The New Testament Doctrine of Baptism;* Ronald C.D. Jasper (ed.), *Worship and the Child*

The Saint Andrew Press: The report, *The Biblical Doctrine of Baptism*

Quotations from the Bible are from *New English Bible*, Second Edition, © 1970, by kind permission of the Oxford and Cambridge University Presses.

Preface

A FEW WORDS of explanation are perhaps required to justify the appearance of yet another book on the subject of infant baptism, about which so much has been written in recent years. W. F. Flemington's major work, *The New Testament Doctrine of Baptism,* is still of great value in understanding the New Testament; Joachim Jeremias and Kurt Aland (in *Infant Baptism in the First Four Centuries* and *Did the Early Church Baptize Infants?* respectively) may be deemed, if not to have settled the issue, to have shown the impossibility of certainty about the exact date when infant baptism began; while such accounts as Geoffrey Wainwright's *Christian Initiation* and *The Water that Divides* by Donald Bridge and David Phypers seem to have covered the whole field effectively.

Yet there is abundant evidence that, despite the immensity of the literature, or because of it, many ministers and others in churches which practise infant baptism have considerable difficulty in coming to terms either with the theology or with the practice of infant baptism in today's society. As a Methodist minister in a circuit appointment, I know some of the difficulties from personal experience, and I have often heard of others from colleagues and friends. When I was asked to write this book, therefore, although I was reluctant to plunge into such 'troubled waters', I felt that this was a challenge which I could not, and should not, refuse.

A good many ministers responded to a request which I made in *The Methodist Recorder* and told me of their views and experiences. Some sent me copies of leaflets which they have produced. Much of what my correspondents had to say has found its way into the book, though I have not thought it right to divulge their names, for reasons which will be obvious. I hope that they will accept these words as an indication of my gratitude to them for supplying me with such useful information. I should also like to acknowledge my indebtedness to the Reverends Donald English, A. Raymond George and John Stacey, who made numerous helpful suggestions, though it should be clearly understood that none of them is to be held responsible for the views expressed in these pages.

NEIL DIXON

November 1978

Introduction

WATER has many uses. A man can wash in it, swim in it, drink it. It supports and sustains life. But it is also lethal. A man can drown in it. Certain precautions ought, therefore, to be taken by those who venture into the sea: the basic skills should be acquired; warning signs along the beach should be noted; the advice of local residents should be heeded.

Anyone who plunges into the troubled waters of the baptism debate needs to have some points of reference if he is not to be caught in the cross-current of opinion or drowned by the tidal waves of argument. This modest contribution to the debate is based on a number of assumptions which the writer believes to be life-lines:

First, history and tradition cannot be ignored. The worship and mission of the Church cannot be re-assessed in any one age without careful reference to Christian history. We need to keep an eye on scripture and tradition. Our study begins, therefore, with an examination of New Testament doctrine and proceeds to examine the circumstances in which infant baptism (sometimes called paedobaptism) began to be practised. We then assess the theological arguments for and against paedobaptism and the relationship between baptism on the one hand and confirmation, conversion and communion on the other. Because this book is written in a Methodist context, we then consider the recently authorized Methodist initiation services.

Second, to state that history and tradition cannot be ignored is not to say that all inherited practices are self-justifying. New occasions may, as the hymn says, teach new duties, time make ancient good uncouth. A thorough assessment of our present-day practice, based on our understanding of modern society, is therefore complementary to and as important as an examination of scripture and tradition. For this reason, Part Two of this book is devoted to the practicalities of the matter.

Third, in a complex debate it is necessary to identify arguments with precision. It would be a serious mistake, for example, to assume that all who opposed the practice of infant baptism did so on the same grounds. Some writers propose arguments against the practice which are unacceptable, even repugnant, to others who oppose it with equal vehemence. And, as Chapter Nine will show, pleas for services in lieu of infant baptism often confuse services of dedication on the one hand with services of thanksgiving and blessing on the other, thus in turn obscuring the purpose for which such services might be thought suitable. Various arguments, then, must be identified, disentangled, and evaluated.

This study, working on the lines suggested above, moves through an examination of the history, theology and liturgy of baptism to a consideration of present-day experience and various possible solutions. In the final chapter, a definite conclusion emerges. The solution proposed in Chapter Ten is not original, nor is it the only possible solution, but the writer offers it for consideration because he has come to believe it to be the best.

It has proved impossible completely to overcome the problem that certain phrases often used in debates about baptism appear judgmental. Thus the present writer speaks of 'indiscriminate' baptism and of 'lax' policy, where other writers prefer the terms 'general' baptism and 'charitable' policy. It is to be hoped that the arguments adduced for and against the various approaches will carry more weight than the terms employed to describe them.

In order to provide consistency throughout the book, certain liberties have been taken with capital letters in some quotations. Lower case letters have been used for words such as 'baptism', and 'thanksgiving'; and ' the Church' refers to the Universal Church as opposed to the local 'church'. Unless otherwise stated, italicized passages in quotations were thus marked by the authors quoted.

PART ONE
Baptism in History and Theology

CHAPTER ONE

The New Testament Doctrine of Baptism

ANY SERIOUS discussion of the meaning and practice of baptism must begin with the New Testament, for in the events to which the scriptures bear witness—in the baptism of Jesus himself and of the early Christians—the origins of the Christian rite are to be found. If we wish to know what baptism means, and if we want to consider the relative merits of infant and believers' baptism, we must begin our inquiry here.

'The reader of the New Testament is confronted immediately with baptism. To avoid it he would have to ignore the events surrounding the beginning of Christ's ministry and the beginning of the Church's life.'[1] There are indeed many New Testament references to the administration of baptism and to its theological significance; but it is important that we should be aware from the outset that the references to practice are often ambiguous (we shall see that it is impossible to be absolutely certain whether or not infants were baptized in New Testament times) and that the theology, in common with New Testament theology in general, is not fully developed. If we look to the New Testament for fully detailed evidence of the baptismal practice of the early Church or for a coherent account of baptismal theology, we are doomed to disappointment. Nevertheless, the New Testament provides much

[1] Donald Bridge and David Phypers, *The Water that Divides,* Inter-Varsity Press, 1977, p.15

valuable information about baptism, and we begin our study by looking at the pointers which it supplies towards a theology of baptism.

Baptism as a rite of cleansing

Christianity developed out of Judaism, a religion in which ceremonies involving water were commonplace. Ritual washing took place in order to recover lost purity—lost, for example, by touching a dead body.[2] Anyone who was thus impure was obliged to engage in ritual washing before he could again take part in worship. It would be inexact to refer to this as 'merely outward' purification, for in Jewish thought body and soul are indissolubly linked. Indeed, there are passages in the Old Testament where acts of washing are clearly interpreted as being of moral significance:

> There is blood on your hands; wash yourselves and be clean. Put away the evil of your deeds, away out of my sight. Cease to do evil and learn to do right.[3]

Whether or not such washings can be considered a direct antecedent of Christian baptism, there can be no doubt that John the Baptist, depicted by the Gospel writers as the Forerunner of Jesus, linked baptism with repentance and cleansing:

> John the Baptist appeared in the wilderness proclaiming a baptism in token of repentance, for the forgiveness of sins; and they flocked to him from the whole Judaean countryside and the city of Jerusalem, and were baptized by him in the River Jordan, confessing their sins.[4]

John stood in the tradition of Hebrew prophets such as Amos, Hosea and Isaiah of Jerusalem in his fierce denunciation of evil behaviour (witness his scathing attack on the Pharisees and Sadducees)[5] and his demand for moral righteousness. He emphasized the need for repentance and for a change in

[2] See Numbers 19:11ff.
[3] Isaiah 1:16f. See also Psalm 51:7 and Ezekiel 36:25
[4] Mark 1:4f.
[5] Matthew 3:7–12

behaviour.[6] Baptism, as John practised it, was 'expressive of a thorough-going moral reformation'.[7]

The symbolism was very impressive. The man who repented, who was genuinely sorry about his former behaviour, came for washing, for cleansing, for the removal of his past, and, having passed through the waters, returned to land to start over again. In Jewish thought there was no concept of a 'mere' symbol, for a symbol contained within itself something of what it represented; we can assume, therefore, that those whom John baptized would see the act of baptism not merely as a symbol of forgiveness but as a means through which God effected their forgiveness. But here we must raise for the first time a question which will continue to engage our attention throughout this study, the relationship between faith and ritual action. It is important to note that a definite response was obviously required of the people who came to John for baptism. They

> needed to be conscious of failure and guilt. They needed to be sufficiently concerned about it to abandon certain kinds of behaviour. They had to show a practical desire for a better way of life.[8]

Thus there is no suggestion here that baptism was an efficacious cleansing rite *ex opere operato*.[9] On the other hand, it would be a gross distortion of biblical thought to suggest that John's baptism was considered to be a 'mere' ritual, devoid of any efficacy.

John's teaching that baptism is a washing away of sin is carried over into Christian baptism. Peter's sermon on the Day of Pentecost challenges his hearers to ask 'What must we do?'. And the answer is:

[6] Matthew 3:8; Luke 3:7–14

[7] W. F. Flemington, *The New Testament Doctrine of Baptism,* S.P.C.K., 1964 edition, p.17

[8] Bridge and Phypers, op. cit., p.16

[9] Here and elsewhere in this book *ex opere operato* is used in its commonly accepted sense to mean 'by reason of the work performed', that is, to denote a mechanical view of the efficacy of the sacraments. I am indebted, however, to A. Raymond George for the information that, in Roman Catholic theology, the phrase means 'by reason of the work done by Christ' and is contrasted with *ex opere operantis* ('by reason of the work done by the celebrant')

> Repent and be baptized, every one of you, in the name of Jesus the Messiah for the forgiveness of your sins.[10]

Ananias is said to have counselled Paul,

> Be baptized at once, with invocation of his name, and wash away your sins.[11]

Repentance is the necessary prelude to baptism, through which sins are washed away and forgiveness effected. The man who is dirty because of sin enters the waters of baptism to become clean. But as with John's baptism, there is no suggestion here of a mechanical process; the willing participation of the baptized is pre-supposed, as are his penitence and his faith.

Three other passages in which baptism is described in terms of cleansing, all of them set in the context of ethical instruction, are worthy of special attention. First, Paul writes to the Corinthians:

> Surely you know that the unjust will never come into possession of the kingdom of God. Make no mistake: no fornicator or idolater . . . will possess the kingdom of God. Such were some of you. But you have been through the purifying waters; you have been dedicated to God and justified through the name of the Lord Jesus and the Spirit of our God.[12]

Here Paul is insisting that Christian conduct must be decisively different from pagan behaviour. Whatever their past lives may have been, the act of baptism had marked an absolute change in the baptized. The old life and the new were separated by the waters of baptism. Flemington has pointed out the importance of this passage because of the way in which it links baptism with the great Pauline doctrines of justification and sanctification.[13] Paul clearly set great store by baptism, and one of the ways in which he understood it was as an act of purification, for the washing away of sin.

[10] Acts 2:37f.
[11] Acts 22:16
[12] Corinthians 6:9ff.
[13] Flemington, op. cit., p.56

Once again, it is in the context of ethical teaching that the writer to the Ephesians exhorts husbands to:

> love your wives, as Christ also loved the Church and gave himself up for it, to consecrate it, cleansing it by water and word, so that he might present the Church to himself all glorious, with no stain or wrinkle or anything of the sort, but holy and without blemish.[14]

In this passage we note the idea that the Church is a community of people who have been cleansed by baptism. The 'word' probably refers to a profession of faith (maybe 'Jesus is Lord') made by the candidate for baptism.[15]

Finally, the writer to the Hebrews says:

> Let us draw near in sincerity of heart and full assurance of faith, our guilty hearts sprinkled clean, our bodies washed with pure water.[16]

This reference to baptism contains an allusion to Old Testament ritual, in which priests were required to purify themselves with water before offering sacrifices[17] and to purify the holy things by sprinkling them with the blood of sacrificial victims.[18] In the thought of the letter to the Hebrews, Christ cleanses his Church by his own blood, and

> this once-for-all cleansing which Christ accomplished on the Cross is applied to us in the once-for-all cleansing in baptism.[19]

The concept of baptism as an act of purification, then, is clearly present in the New Testament.

Baptism as participation in Christ's death and resurrection
The metaphor of washing and cleansing, although common in the New Testament, is not the only way in which baptism is

[14] Ephesians 5:25ff.
[15] See Flemington, op. cit., p.124
[16] Hebrews 10:22
[17] See Numbers 8:7
[18] See Leviticus 16:14, 18f.
[19] *The Biblical Doctrine of Baptism*, a Study Document of the Special Commission of the Church of Scotland on Baptism, The Saint Andrew Press, 1958, p.23

there understood. If a man may wash in water, he may also drown in it. Water cleanses; it also kills. This truth led Paul to write about baptism in a very compelling way as participation in the death of Christ, and in his resurrection:

> Shall we persist in sin, so that there may be all the more grace? No, no! We died to sin: how can we live in it any longer? Have you forgotten that when we were baptized into union with Christ Jesus we were baptized into his death? By baptism we were buried with him, and lay dead, in order that, as Christ was raised from the dead in the splendour of the Father, so also we might set our feet upon the new path of life. For if we have become incorporate with him in a death like his, we shall also be one with him in a resurrection like his.[20]

While it is no doubt true that Paul is here using baptism as 'a useful model with which to demonstrate the true nature of response to divine grace'[21] it is difficult to resist the conclusion that, for Paul, baptism represented a real and dramatic transition from one way of life, to which the baptized person 'died', to another. The actions of baptism are the means through which the believer participates in the events by which God wrought mankind's salvation in Jesus Christ. In the act of baptism, the believer is identified with Christ's death and resurrection. He is plunged into water, water in which a man may drown: he dies then, as Christ died. He is held under the water for a time, buried as Christ was buried. Then he comes out of the water, emerging to begin a new life, resurrected as Christ was resurrected.

> Paul reaches the height of his christocentric baptismal theology in the conception of 'dying and rising with Christ'. . . In baptism the believer in Christ is drawn into the Christ event; he accompanies his Lord through death to resurrection . . . It is not simply a question of remembrance and becoming like him, but rather a participation in Christ's cross and resurrection, so that everything that Christ went through for our salvation also happens to the baptized, and he thus obtains the fruit of Christ's dying. These statements . . . are founded on a Semitic idea, according to which

[20] Romans 6:1–6
[21] Donald English in *Epworth Review,* January 1974, p.63

the founder of a people is inseparably bound up with those who are joined to him; he represents and takes the place of his followers, and these again share his destiny.[22]

As with the metaphor of cleansing, so too in the concept of dying and rising with Christ we see that baptism marks an absolute separation between one way of life and another:

> Paul's assertion is that what happened for us in the death and resurrection of Christ has happened to us in baptism, committing us to a personal death to sin and a personal resurrection to newness of life. This is a change which controls our whole life ever afterwards. Our personal dying and rising with Christ are not our own work, but Christ's life-giving death and resurrection life now active in us (cf. among many other passages Galatians 2:19f.), for he who died and rose again is himself really, and not merely symbolically, present to the baptized, uniting them to himself in their faith and life.[23]

The idea of participation in Christ's death and resurrection is not confined to Romans, but recurs in other epistles. For example, in a passage of moral instruction in Colossians, we read:

> Did you not die with Christ and pass beyond the reach of the elemental spirits of the universe? Then why behave as though you were still living the life of the world? . . . Were you not raised to life with Christ? Then aspire to the realm above, where Christ is, seated at the right hand of God, and let your thoughts dwell on that higher realm, not on this earthly life. I repeat, you died; and now your life lies hidden with Christ in God. When Christ, who is our life, is manifested, then you too will be manifested with him in glory. Then put to death those parts of you which belong to the earth . . .[24]

This passage, which so closely follows the imagery of Romans 6, makes it abundantly clear that, in Pauline thought, baptism is the means whereby the individual may be identified with

---

[22] Rudolf Schnackenburg, *Baptism in the Thought of St. Paul,* translated by G. R. Beasley-Murray, Basil Blackwell, 1964, pp.205f.
[23] *The Biblical Doctrine of Baptism,* p.26
[24] Colossians 2:20; 3:1–5

Christ in the supreme events of mankind's salvation, the death and resurrection of Christ. This identification leads to a new life,[25] it has eschatological significance,[26] and it imposes moral obligations on the baptized:

> Christians have already to live according to the ethical implications of their baptism. Through having shared Christ's death and resurrection the baptized are henceforward dead to sin and alive to righteousness. The indicative is the basis for an imperative: Christians are to lay hold of what is already given to them, they are to become what they are.[27]

Baptism as incorporation into Christ and the Church

We have just observed the powerful way in which Paul describes baptism as an identification of the believer with Christ. Another way of looking at this is to see it as a process of initiation or incorporation of the believer into Christ. 'We were baptized into union with Christ Jesus'[28] 'Baptized into union with him, you have all put on Christ as a garment'.[29] The reference to a garment is an allusion to the robe which the newly baptized person would put on after emerging from the water. The Christian has 'put on' Christ; he is now one with Christ, or, to use a characteristic Pauline phrase, he is 'in Christ'.

He is also initiated, or incorporated, into the Christian community. Jewish proselyte baptism was probably the principal antecedent of John's baptism, itself the direct antecedent of Christian baptism.[30] Initiation into Judaism was its main purpose; it was administered to Gentiles who wished to become Jews. Proselyte baptism meant an abandonment of the old way of life and an acceptance of a new way. The proselyte took upon himself 'the yoke of the Law', submitting himself to the moral obligations of Judaism. He was cleansed from defilement by ritual washing in the waters of baptism. In the end, after circumcision and baptism, the proselyte was

---

[25] See below, pp.21f.
[26] See below, pp.24f.
[27] Geoffrey Wainwright, *Christian Initiation*, Lutterworth Press, 1969, p.11
[28] Romans 6:3
[29] Galatians 3:27
[30] See Flemington, op. cit., pp.4–11

regarded as being 'in all respects an Israelite'.[31] Formerly he had lived outside the Covenant community; now he belonged to it. He had been initiated. He had been incorporated into Israel.

By direct descent, this notion of incorporation into a community and initiation into a new religion found its way into Christianity. In Christian baptism a man is received into the community of Jesus, the Body of Christ:

> Christ is like a single body with its many limbs and organs, which, many as they are, together make up one body. For indeed we were all brought into one body by baptism, in the one Spirit, whether we are Jews or Greeks, whether slaves or free men, and that one Holy Spirit was poured out for all of us to drink.[32]

Thus baptism is entry into the Church, incorporation into the Body of Christ. It signifies the unity of the Church; its members are joined to Christ by baptism and are therefore joined to one another. Social status or previous religious allegiance cannot divide them, for these things are of no account compared with their common place in the new community, the Body of Christ, to which baptism has admitted them.

Baptism as regeneration
> Jesus answered, 'In truth I tell you, unless a man has been born over again he cannot see the kingdom of God. . . . No one can enter the kingdom of God without being born from water and spirit'.[33]

This excerpt from the Fourth Gospel's account of a conversation between Jesus and Nicodemus has not always been understood to include an allusion to baptism, though 'most commentators take the word "water" as an obvious reference to Christian baptism'.[34] The concept of regeneration or rebirth was not unfamiliar to the Jews. A baptized proselyte was spoken of by the Rabbis as having the status of a newborn

---

[31] *Babylonian Talmud,* quoted in Flemington, op. cit., p.7
[32] 1 Corinthians 12:12f.
[33] John 3:3, 5
[34] Flemington, op. cit., p.86

child.[35] It seems highly probable that, for the writer of the Fourth Gospel, baptism in water combined with the activity of the Holy Spirit is the means whereby the individual is reborn. This is entirely consistent with other New Testament passages, some of which we have already considered. Paul's conception of baptism as an identification of the baptized with Christ, for example, includes the idea that baptism inaugurates a new (resurrection) life; it is, therefore, a rebirth. The idea of baptismal washing also conveys a definite suggestion that an old life has been washed away and a new life begun. If there are relatively few passages which speak directly of baptismal regeneration, many others imply it. But the concept of rebirth is unmistakably present in Titus:

> Not for any good deeds of our own, but because he was merciful, he (God) saved us through the water of rebirth and the renewing power of the Holy Spirit.[36]

Nowhere, of course, is it suggested that water-baptism effects regeneration *ex opere operato*. On the contrary, regeneration is the sovereign act of God, who is active in the sacrament through the Holy Spirit. The passages quoted from John and Titus both make this clear. It is God who gives new birth, just as elsewhere it is God who incorporates men into Christ and the Church, who enables them to participate in Christ's death and resurrection, and who washes away sin.

Baptism as the seal of the Spirit
We have already noted several passages in which the activity of the Holy Spirit is associated with baptism.[37] We must now look at three other passages which many commentators believe to be references to baptism, though baptism is not explicitly mentioned. All these passages are related to the 'seal of the Spirit'.

In Jewish thought, circumcision was regarded as the seal or mark of God's possession of his people, the attestation of his

[35] *The Biblical Doctrine of Baptism*, p.33. For an account of the significance of Jewish proselyte baptism and a defence of the view that it was practised sufficiently early to be an antecedent of Christian baptism, see Flemington, op. cit., pp.4–11
[36] Titus 3:6
[37] See John 3:3,5; 1 Corinthians 12:12f.; 6:9ff.; Titus 3:5

ownership.[38] Circumcision was, of course, the initiation rite of Judaism, as baptism is of Christianity, and it is suggested that the Old Testament concept of 'sealing' is applied to baptism in the verses quoted below:

> It is God who has set his seal upon us, and as a pledge of what is to come has given the Spirit to dwell in our hearts.[39]

> And you too, when you had heard the message of the truth, the good news of your salvation, and had believed it, became incorporate in Christ and received the seal of the promised Holy Spirit; and that Spirit is the pledge that we shall enter upon our heritage.[40]

> And do not grieve the Holy Spirit of God, for that Spirit is the seal with which you were marked for the day of our final liberation.[41]

It might be argued that the 'seal' is in fact the gift of the Holy Spirit in some context other than baptism.[42] After all, in none of these passages is there a direct reference to water-baptism. Against this it must be said that the first of the passages, 2 Corinthians 1:22, associates but does not identify the sealing and the indwelling of the Holy Spirit, that reference to the Spirit in connection with baptism is extremely frequent elsewhere,[43] and that 'sealing' was used by Christian writers in the second century in a way that suggests that it had become a common synonymn for baptism.[44] G. W. H. Lampe, in a major examination of the term, reaches the conclusion that:

> the connection between the 'sealing with the Spirit' . . . and the sacrament of baptism is so close that the one can be regarded as the thing signified by the other.[45]

[38] See Genesis 17:10–14
[39] 2 Corinthians 1:22
[40] Ephesians 1:13f.
[41] Ephesians 4:30
[42] For a discussion of the view that 'sealing with the Spirit' refers to a primitive form of confirmation, see below, pp.73ff.
[43] See the passages cited in note 37 above, and also Mark 1:9ff. and parallels in the other Gospels
[44] See Flemington, op. cit., p.66
[45] G. W. H. Lampe, *The Seal of the Spirit,* Longmans, Green and Company, 1951, p.4

This concept is best regarded as another way of describing initiation or incorporation, though it has the added reference to the work of the Holy Spirit. Through the Spirit's action in baptism a person comes to share in the New Covenant, just as he might have been admitted to the Old Covenant by means of circumcision. The baptized are 'sealed' as God's possession.

Baptism and eschatology

John the Baptist accompanied his baptisms with preaching about the coming Messianic Age:[46]

> John declares that his baptism cannot be compared with that which Messiah will effect by fire and Spirit; yet John's rite is undeniably eschatological. The baptized are prepared for survival: they will pass safely through the Messianic storm; they are wheat ready for Messiah's garner, and they know already they will find mercy in the Day of wrath. By baptism they have entered so far as possible into the imminent New Age: they are ready for it, look towards it, are assured of their place within it, taste by anticipation its blessings. In this way baptism gains in John's hands a new dimension of initiatory meaning—as initiation into the eschatological fulfilment, into the Messianic Age, and into the prepared Messianic community, the nucleus of the coming Kingdom.[47]

Not surprisingly, similar eschatological concepts found a place in the Christian understanding of baptism. Several of the passages which we have examined in other connections sound an eschatological note.[48] The new age was dawning; the pouring out of the Spirit in the Messianic Age was taking place; and baptism was the means whereby an individual was incorporated into Messiah's kingdom and given a pledge of his place in the new order:

> The baptized has entered upon the New Age, has seen the New Day, and belongs therefore already to the eschatological scene. He has tasted of the powers of the world to come, and stands, on

[46] See Matthew 3:1–12

[47] R. E. O. White, *The Biblical Doctrine of Initiation,* Hodder and Stoughton, 1960, p.87

[48] See, for example, Ephesians 1:13.f; 4:30; 5:26.f; Colossians 3:3.f; Titus 3:4–8

the far side of baptism, already within the new order. For those stepping with faith into the immersion-pool, the time is fulfilled and the kingdom of God is at hand; for those rising from it, the kingdom has come and is within them.[49]

Redemption is both past and future event. At the cross and resurrection redemption has been effected: at the *parousia* it will be brought to completion. So the Kingdom has come, yet awaits its full manifestation. So the Spirit has been given, yet remains in us the first-fruits of the inheritance. So the Church is the Body of Christ, yet remains under the Cross. So the Christian has been justified, yet awaits final salvation. Baptism is thus a sacrament of inaugurated eschatology. It is grounded in the atoning work of Christ which it applies and extends. It looks towards the *parousia*.[50]

The baptism of Jesus

We must not overlook the most significant of all references to baptism in the New Testament, those which relate to the baptism of Jesus himself by John the Baptist. All four Gospels bear witness to this event, and there is little support for the view that the incident is unhistorical.[51] But why did Jesus's baptism take place, and what significance did the early Church attach to it?

The event is presented as part of Jesus's preparation for his public ministry; indeed it can be described as his acceptance of God's will for him, his commitment to the tasks of Sonship. In his baptism Jesus identifies himself with sinful humanity. Matthew tells us that John was understandably reluctant to baptize Jesus, in whom he recognized no need for cleansing.[52] But Jesus will not stand aloof from the new movement which John has inaugurated; still less will he detach himself from sinful humanity. In his obedience and his humiliation, he is conscious of his divine Sonship and of the Spirit of God coming upon him.[53] These elements distinguish the baptism of Jesus from other baptisms performed by John. Sonship of

[49] White, op. cit., p.272
[50] *Initiation and Eucharist,* Essays by the Joint Liturgical Group, edited by Neville Clark and Ronald C. D. Jasper, S.P.C.K., 1972, p.12
[51] See Flemington, op. cit., pp.25ff., White, op. cit., pp.91ff.
[52] Matthew 3:14
[53] Matthew 3:16f.

God and the gift of the Spirit are new associations, though, as we have seen, both of them were to influence the Christian understanding of baptism.

There is another use of the word 'baptism' in the Synoptic Gospels which is of special significance:

> Can you drink the cup that I drink, or be baptized with the baptism I am baptized with?[54]

> I have a baptism to undergo, and what constraint I am under until the ordeal is over![55]

Here baptism refers to the approaching death of Jesus and indicates that his death will be the act that inaugurates the Kingdom, Christ's fuller activity, 'unfettered by the restrictions of the earthly ministry'[56] If these words faithfully represent the teaching of Jesus, it may well be that the connection, so characteristic of Paul's teaching, between baptism and death (and resurrection) had its origin in the thought of Jesus himself.

Baptism, grace, and faith

The centre of Paul's theology is Christ, crucified and risen. In the cross and the resurrection God has acted to redeem mankind. Mankind cannot save itself, nor can a man earn God's favour. Salvation is bestowed upon those who do not deserve it, only because God is gracious. The benefits of Christ's death and resurrection can be appropriated only by faith. This teaching, which asserts that a man is forgiven and received into God's family by means of a response of faith to God's grace, is so important in Pauline thought that some commentators have been inclined to play down Paul's teaching about baptism as a means of incorporation into Christ and as participation in Christ's death and resurrection.

But this is to misunderstand the relationship between baptism and faith. In the first place, to do justice to New Testament thought, we must make it clear that it is neither by submitting to baptism nor by professing faith that a person

[54] Mark 10:38
[55] Luke 12:50
[56] Flemington, op.cit., p.32

26

can be saved; it is by the gracious action of God, whose reconciling work in Christ has made salvation possible. God's grace is prior both to man's faith and to the Church's action in baptizing. Secondly, in Paul's thought and elsewhere, baptism and faith belong together. Jewish thought, which greatly influenced Christian theology, recognized no distinction between body and soul; God's grace demanded a response from the whole man. The early Church could not have conceived of a distinction between the bodily act of baptism and a subjective response of faith. The two were inseparable. Thirdly, and this is an issue which will be of significance for us in subsequent chapters, baptism in New Testament times was normally (or, as some would say, invariably) administered to adult converts. Thus:

> the question of the validity of baptism apart from the conscious assent of the baptized person does not arise. Nor would it have been natural for Paul and his contemporaries to consider the question whether faith without baptism made a man a member of Christ's Body, while the case of a person seeking baptism without faith (however rudimentary) would seem to him too abnormal to deserve notice.[57]

As with John's baptism, so too in Christian baptism, a response was called for from those who came to be baptized. Repentance was a pre-requisite; and God's prevenient grace was at work in evoking that response. The divine offer was made, variously described as new life, rebirth, resurrection, eternal life, participation in the new creation, entry into the kingdom of God. God's grace alone made this offer possible. The man who repented would then make a further response by believing and by being baptized. It is a peculiarly modern—and unbiblical—way of looking at things to refer to faith as an inward response and to submission to baptism as an external response, or to consider faith to be the important thing, of which baptism is a 'mere' symbol. Such distinctions had no meaning in the first century. That man was 'in Christ' who believed and was baptized. The New Testament cannot help us to decide whether the one could be valid without the

[57] C. H. Dodd, *The Epistle of Paul to the Romans*, Fontana Edition, 1959, p.107

other, for the action and its meaning are one in biblical thought. 'Baptism and faith together constitute the individual's response to God'.[58]

Summary

In this brief sketch of the New Testament understanding of baptism we have discovered a number of important concepts which we shall have to bear in mind in our subsequent discussions. These may be summarized thus:

1. The grace of God and his mighty acts of redemption in the life, death and resurrection of Jesus Christ provide the context from which Christian baptism takes its meaning, and alone make it possible.

2. Baptism is inseparably linked with faith. The New Testament has nothing to say about baptism without faith or faith without baptism.

3. Baptism is closely associated with the activity of the Holy Spirit, who came upon Jesus at his baptism and who is described as indwelling and sealing those who are baptized.

4. Baptism is a means of cleansing. Unlike Jewish purification ceremonies, it is not repeated, but symbolizes once and for all the cleansing from sin which is available as a result of Christ's work, to those who are 'in Christ'.

5. Baptism is a new beginning. This may be described as a rebirth or as a sharing in Christ's death and resurrection. The powerful symbol of entering the water, being immersed in it, and emerging from it represents not merely a change of status but also a change of life-style. Thus the great Pauline doctrines of justification and sanctification, both closely associated with faith, are also closely related to baptism.

6. Baptism signifies that a person belongs to God (as did circumcision in the Old Covenant) and that he is included in God's kingdom, now and in the future.

7. Like Jewish proselyte baptism, Christian baptism signifies entry into a community. The Church is made up of the baptized. Baptism, as a result, is conceived to be a mark of the unity of the Church; and there are to be no racial or social distinctions among the baptized.

[58] Bridge and Phypers, op. cit., p.28

CHAPTER TWO

The Practice of Infant Baptism

IN THE LAST chapter, we looked at some of the major theological statements which the New Testament makes about baptism. We now turn to the much more controversial subject, the origin of the practice of infant baptism. In looking at the New Testament doctrine, we have quite correctly assumed that in the early Church the baptism of believers was the norm. We must now ask whether it was more than a norm. Was it an invariable rule, or were infants baptized in apostolic times? If they were, on what understanding were they baptized? If they were not, when did the practice of infant baptism begin?

The view that infants were baptized in New Testament times has been argued with great cogency by Professor Jeremias,[1] who has built up a composite case from the rather fragmentary evidence supplied by the New Testament and other sources. The following is a summary of the main points of Jeremias's argument:

1. Jewish proselyte baptism is regarded by many scholars as the most important antecedent of Christian baptism.[2] It was the means by which Gentiles who desired to become Jews were admitted, after circumcision, into the community of Israel. If a proselyte had children, it was customary for them to be circumcised and baptized too.[3] The concept of the solidarity of the family was so strong that the inability of

[1] Joachim Jeremias, *Infant Baptism in the First Four Centuries,* S.C.M. Press, 1960
[2] See Flemington, op. cit., pp.4–11
[3] Jeremias, op. cit., pp.37f.

children to make promises on their own behalf was not deemed important.

> In view of the close connection between primitive Christian baptism and proselyte baptism . . . it must be assumed that in the question of infant baptism also the Christian baptismal ritual corresponded to that of proselyte baptism, i.e. that with the admission of Gentiles to Christianity children of every age, including infants, were baptized also.[4]

2. There are a number of references in the New Testament to the baptism of 'households'. One must serve as an example of the rest.[5] Acts 16:33 tells of the Philippian jailor who was baptized, together with his whole family. Earlier in the same story is a reference to the salvation of the 'household'. According to Jeremias, everyone living in a house, including servants, was considered to belong to the household.[6] It therefore seems reasonable to assume that, in at least some of the households which are referred to in connection with baptism, there were young children or infants who were baptized along with the other members of the household. Jeremias argues that the 'oikos' formula ('oikos' is Greek for 'household') was adopted from Old Testament cultic language, in which it definitely embraced all residents in a house, including infants, and that, had Paul or Luke been writing about circumstances in which only adults were baptized, they would not have used the 'oikos' formula.[7]

3. Jeremias reaches the same conclusion, that 'whole household' means precisely what it says, on the grounds that the solidarity of the family was a strongly held concept in biblical times.[8] Modern thinking, with its strong emphasis on individuality, is quite foreign to biblical thought, according to which all important issues, particularly in relation to religion, were decided by the head of a family, whose decision was binding on the other members. The circumcision of male infants is rarely mentioned in the Old Testament; it is taken

[4] Ibid., p.39
[5] See also 1 Corinthians 1:16; Acts 16:15; Acts 18:8
[6] Jeremias, op. cit., p.20
[7] Ibid., pp.20f.
[8] Ibid., pp.22f.

for granted. So, in the New Testament, the idea of family solidarity was so prevalent that it was not necessary to mention that infants were baptized.

4. The arguments which we have thus far listed refer to the alleged baptism of the children of adults who were converted to Christianity. What of children born to Christian parents? Jeremias finds 'no special evidence for the baptism of Christian children'[9] in the New Testament itself, but he builds up a case for it from other sources. In approximately A.D. 168, Bishop Polycarp of Smyrna is said to have refused to revile Christ with the words, 'For eighty-six years I have served him'.The long period of time involved suggests that Polycarp was dating his Christian service from his baptism as an infant, which in turn suggests that infant baptism was taking place around A.D. 80. Justin Martyr, around A.D. 150, refers to men and women aged sixty or seventy years who have been disciples of Christ from childhood. the Greek word which we translate 'have been disciples' has strong baptismal associations, and therefore suggests that children were baptized in the years following A.D. 80. Origen, writing in the first half of the third century, refers to infant baptism as an apostolic practice; and Tertullian, a few decades earlier, in opposing infant baptism and counselling that children should not be baptized until they were old enough to speak for themselves seems to be opposing a well-established practice, for he nowhere suggests that paedobaptism is an innovation, an argument which he could scarcely have failed to use against it if it had been.[10]

Jeremias had built up a strong cumulative case to support his contention that infant baptism was practised in New Testament times; but within a few years a powerful reply was forthcoming from Professor Kurt Aland,[11] which we summarize below:

1. The argument from Jewish proselyte baptism is inconclusive. Most of the missionary expansion of the early Church

[9] Ibid., p.55
[10] These illustrations are only a few of the pieces of patristic evidence cited by Jeremias, op. cit., pp.59–86
[11] Kurt Aland, *Did the Early Church Baptize Infants?* S.C.M. Press, 1963

occurred in regions where proselyte baptism was unfamiliar; and the rite is so different in meaning from Christian baptism that it is going too far to assume that infant baptism was carried over from the one to the other.

2. The 'oikos' formula is subjected to careful scrutiny by Aland, who thinks it improbable that such a formula, conveying the meaning which Jeremias suggests, was in common use.[12] The passages cited by Jeremias as examples of the 'oikos' formula are at best inconclusive evidence for paedobaptism and

> one thing is indisputable: nowhere in connection with the oikos-passages in the New Testament is a child or an infant expressly named, let alone its baptism.[13]

3. The argument about family solidarity is equally inconclusive. It is essentially an argument from silence, asserting that infant baptism is not explicitly mentioned because its practice was taken for granted. A more obvious line of reasoning would be that infant baptism is not mentioned because it did not occur.

4. Aland also finds flaws in Jeremias's citations from patristic sources. First he refers to evidence which Jeremias fails to cite, all of which comes from the period A.D. 100 to 150. The *Didache* has a chapter devoted to baptism, which makes it clear that a period of instruction and a time of fasting preceded the administration of the rite; this would seem to exclude infants, who could neither be instructed nor expected to fast.[14] *The Shepherd of Hermas* and the *Letter of Barnabas* both refer to the past sins and defilements which baptism washes away, a fact which suggests that these documents are thinking only of adults as candidates for baptism.[15] The *Apology* of Aristides, which belongs to the same period, appears to indicate the baptism of children, though not infants:

> They instruct the servants and maids, or the children when any of them have such, that they become Christians, on account of the

12 Ibid., pp.87–94
13 Ibid., p.94
14 Ibid., pp.53f.
15 Ibid., p.54

love which they have for them. And when they have become Christians they call them brothers without distinction.[16]

Thus children, it is suggested, were baptized when they were old enough to know what they were doing, and thereafter were regarded as full Christians, despite their youth.

Second, Aland differs from Jeremias about the value of the evidence which the latter in fact cites. The men and women of sixty or seventy years mentioned by Justin were not necessarily baptized in infancy, nor, despite his great age, are Polycarp's words sufficient evidence that he was baptized as an infant.[17] Origen's spirited defence of the practice of infant baptism proves only that the practice was both known and attacked early in the third century; there is no indication that Origen had any evidence for his assertion that paedobaptism was an apostolic tradition.[18] And Tertullian's polemic can in fact be interpreted as an attack on an innovation.[19]

The fact that two leading scholars have reached opposite conclusions ought to indicate to us how ambiguous is the evidence with which we have to deal. Historical study seems unable to answer the question whether or not infant baptism took place in the first two centuries. There is insufficient clear evidence for us to be sure one way or the other.

It is sometimes suggested that the debate about the validity of paedobaptism could be settled if we had incontrovertible evidence either that the early Church baptized infants or that it did not. But this is not necessarily the case. It is indeed possible to argue that, if the early Church baptized infants, the Church must remain committed to the practice until the end of time; or that, if the early Church did not, the practice is an unjustified deviation from the New Testament norm. But there are other possibilities to consider, which will engage our attention in subsequent chapters. Suppose, on the one hand, that the early Church did baptize infants; is it not at least conceivable that the cultural and sociological factors which the Church encounters in the twentieth century might make

[16] Ibid., p.57
[17] Ibid., pp.71ff.
[18] Ibid., pp.47f.
[19] Ibid., pp.61–69

paedobaptism no longer acceptable? Or, on the other hand, if we suppose that infant baptism was an innovation in the second or third century, could it not be that the Church was right at that time in making this innovation and, rather than betraying its trust, was responding appropriately to new circumstances?

Since we are without incontrovertible evidence for the early Church, we are obliged to ask such questions, to try to find out what significance was attached to infant baptism from the earliest period at which we know for certain that it was practised, and to assess its appropriateness in the social circumstances of our own day. Even if we could be sure about New Testament baptismal practice, we should still have to subject it to the same sort of scrutiny if we were to justify either infant baptism or believers' baptism as the norm in the twentieth century.

From Tertullian to Constantine

There can be no doubt that infant baptism was practised at the beginning of the third century. Tertullian could not have opposed the practice otherwise. But we do not know how widespread it was; nor can we make unchallengeable claims about its antiquity. Yet towards the middle of the third century, Origen in Palestine referred to paedobaptism as the custom of the Church, a fact which, taken together with evidence from Hippolytus in Rome and Tertullian in North Africa, suggests that infant baptism was common over a wide area, although it seems not to have been practised universally.[20] From the third century onwards, the evidence for paedobaptist practice becomes much more abundant.

It is possible to reconstruct the meaning which was attached to infant baptism at this time, and it is important that we should do so whether or not we believe that the practice began in the third century. Aland, who is of the opinion that infant baptism was first administered in the late second century or in the early years of the third, suggests two reasons for its introduction. First, the Church grew rapidly during the first 200 years of its existence, largely because of the influx of converts who were mainly adult. 'It was only after the Church

[20] Ibid., pp.100f.

had attained a certain strength that the "inner"growth, i.e. the increase in the number of Christians through children born among them, began numerically to play a significant role.'[21] But at the end of the second century, the church grew more rapidly than ever and 'with the increasing strength of the Church the absolute number of children born in it also greatly increased, and their "belonging" to the Church, i.e. their baptism, becomes an ever greater problem'.[22] This explanation, however, leaves many questions unanswered; while it is no doubt true that a greater number of children might step up the demand for baptism, there must always have been infants born to Christian parents. Was the demand for their baptism ignored when there were fewer of them? If so, on what grounds? And if there were good grounds for refusing the demands then, why were the demands met later? Was it only force of numbers that won the case for infant baptism? (It would indeed be possible to turn this suggestion by Aland into an argument against his view that infant baptism started in the late second or early third century: if the Church grew mainly by the influx of converted adults and only minimally because of children born to Christian parents, it is not surprising that we hear much of the baptism of the former and little of the baptism of the latter.)

But Aland himself acknowledges that his first explanation 'remains external, and by itself is insufficient. An inner motive must be added.'[23] This inner motive he traces to the development of the doctrine of original sin. Tertullian had questioned both the necessity and the wisdom of baptizing infants: 'Why hurries the age of innocence to the remission of sins?'[24] Aland explain's Tertullian's point of view:

> So long as it is believed that children are without sin, infant baptism is not needed. For baptism is a bath of cleansing, in which a man is washed clean from his sins. If a child born to Christian parents is sinless, it does not need this bath of cleansing.[25]

[21] Ibid., p.102
[22] Ibid., p.103
[23] Ibid.
[24] Quoted in J. Stevenson, *A New Eusebius*, S.P.C.K., 1965, p.185
[25] Aland, op. cit., p.104

Aland maintains that belief in the innocence and sinlessness of infants was not the monopoly of Tertullian; it can be traced back to Paul,[26] and continued to be urged as late as A.D. 411 by Pelagius.[27] But a different estimate of the state of children was gaining ground, which in turn implied a different approach to infant baptism. Thus Origen asserts that 'no one is pure from stain, yea though he be but one day old',[28] and a little later, Cyprian of Carthage declares that a new-born child

> has not sinned, except that, being born after the flesh according to Adam, he has contracted the contagion of the ancient death at its earliest birth: yet on this very account he approaches the more easily to the reception of the forgiveness of sins, because it is not his own sins that are forgiven him but the sins of another.[29]

This is a fairly early expression of the doctrine of original sin, which was to gain considerable ground until it received its classic exposition in the work of Augustine. On Aland's view, this doctrine gave rise to the practice of infant baptism (because infants were born with the taint of original sin it was essential that they should be cleansed from the taint by baptism); but even if infant baptism had been practised earlier, it is clear that Origen, Cyprian and others used original sin as an argument in favour of paedobaptism, and that this argument increasingly carried weight.

Whether or not we agree with Aland that infant baptism was a second- or third-century innovation, then, there is value in his account of the early understanding of the practice. At whatever period it started, infant baptism would receive strong support from parents who recognized that their children, whom Paul had enjoined them to bring up 'in the Lord',[30] belonged to the Christian Family. Their case was further strengthened by the development of the doctrine of original sin.

On the other hand, another doctrine was also gaining

[26] Ibid.
[27] Ibid. For further evidence, see ibid., pp.105–108
[28] Quoted ibid., p.103
[29] Quoted ibid.
[30] Ephesians 6:4

ground. Tertullian, who opposed not only infant baptism but also the hasty baptism of widows and virgins, did so because he believed that at least some post-baptismal sins were unforgivable.[31] He referred to baptism as a burden, which it is less dangerous to postpone than to obtain. By the fourth century, this view was widely held and led to frequent postponements of baptism.[32] Many believed that the ideal time to be baptized was immediately before death.

Throughout the period we have been considering, Christianity remained a minority religion within the Roman Empire, its members tolerated at certain times, persecuted at others. The Church was a community which people joined by believers' baptism following conversion or by infant baptism in the case of children born to Christian parents or converts. There is, of course, no suggestion that parents other than committed Christians presented their children for baptism; the relationship between the Church and society was such that presentations of this sort would be inconceivable. The visible Church had clearly defined limits. But, with the conversion of the Emperor Constantine, the relationship between Church and society was to change dramatically, and the practice of baptism, among many other things, was to change with it.

From Constantine to the Reformation
The conversion of Constantine is one of the great watersheds of Christian history. No longer a minority religion, Christianity found itself the official religion of the Empire. In the centuries that followed, Christians ceased to be persecuted and sometimes became persecutors. A link was established between Church and state which profoundly affected the subsequent development of the Church. Eventually, 'Christendom' came into being and infant baptism rapidly became the norm. Adult converts were still baptized when a country was 'converted' to Christianity—Charlemagne 'converted' many people from paganism by offering them the choice of

---

[31] See Stevenson, op. cit., p.185
[32] Jeremias, op. cit., p.88 refers to several illustrious children of Christian parents who were not baptized until they were adults. They include Ambrose, Augustine, Basil the Great and Jerome

baptism or execution. But after the initial period of mass conversion, infant baptism took the place of believers' baptism as the norm. To be born into Christendom was to be born a Christian, and to be born a Christian was to be baptized as an infant.

This change is very important. During the first three centuries of the Church's existence, believers' baptism had been the normative means of initiation. Now believers' baptism became increasingly rare.

Also during the period under consideration, the ancient rite of initiation disintegrated in the Western Church,[33] though not in the East. At least as early as the end of the second century, it was customary for baptism to be accompanied by anointing with oil and laying on of hands, and followed by first communion. In this rite the bishop took part. When the size of the Church increased dramatically, however, difficulties arose. There were insufficient bishops to preside at baptisms, not least because it was deemed necessary to baptize infants within a few days of birth. Local priests were therefore empowered to administer baptism, but the acts of chrismation and laying on of hands were deferred until the next visit of the bishop. This separation of baptism and what came to be known as confirmation was originally made on the grounds of expediency, but in due course it came to be felt that, because confirmation was not normally administered to infants, it was right that it should not be. What had been necessary for practical reasons hardened by usage into a rule: confirmation was to be administered to no one under the age of seven years.[34] First communion also was deferred until the age of discretion, especially after the doctrine of transubstantiation, established in the twelfth and thirteenth centuries, made the possibility of accidents with the Host, particularly likely if small children communicated, completely unacceptable.

Although our concern in this book is primarily with baptism, we must not forget that there was originally only one rite of initiation, which included not only water-baptism but also

[33] For a thorough account of the disintegration, see J. D. C. Fisher. *Christian Initiation: Baptism in the Medieval West,* S.P.C.K., 1965

[34] This view did not go unchallenged. See Fisher, op.cit., pp.135f.

what we now know as confirmation, and which was followed by admission to the eucharist. The Western disintegration of the primitive rite raises a number of questions about the relationship between baptism and confirmation and first communion, which we shall examine in Chapter Four.

The Reformation

At the time of the Protestant Reformation, infant baptism had been the norm for centuries. In the West it was administered to infants within a few days of birth; confirmation by a bishop took place several years later. Paedobaptism was firmly established, although a number of sects, deemed by the Catholic Church to be heretical, practised believers' baptism.[35] The Reformation constituted the greatest upheaval in Western Christianity since the time of Constantine. Almost every doctrine and practice of the Church came under intense scrutiny. Baptism was not exempted.

Most of the great Reformers were paedobaptists. Martin Luther, John Calvin and Ulrich Zwingli all upheld the practice and vigorously defended it, although Zwingli had once had doubts about its propriety.[36] Others, however, rejected paedobaptism.

For it was at the time of the Reformation that the great movement which we call 'Anabaptism' came into being. The Anabaptists were disparate groups spread around Europe, all of whom opposed infant baptism:

> Political revolutionaries and anti-trinitarian mystics were lumped together in popular thinking with simple evangelical believers who wished to take the Reformation to what they believed to be its scriptural and logical conclusion.[37]

Some Anabaptists, indeed, had very strange life-styles and very wild notions, but others were serious students of the scriptures who believed that, because they could find only believers' baptism in the New Testament, believers' rather than infant baptism should be the rule. So they 're-baptized' (which is what their name means) those who had been bap-

---

[35] See Bridge and Phypers, op. cit., pp.86–94
[36] Ibid., pp.95–124
[37] Ibid., p.97

tized in infancy but who now professed personal faith. Anabaptism is represented at its best in the life and work of the Dutch Reformer, Menno Simons, whose Mennonite churches survive to this day.[38] If we disregard the lunatic fringe, Anabaptism can be seen as a plea for a regenerate church membership. 'Sacralism', that concept of a Christian state which Christendom had fostered, had, in the Anabaptists' opinion, distorted the nature of the Church. Baptism was meant to be an outward sign of a man's faith already operative and God's grace already imparted. It was to be administered, not to infants, not even to the infants of believers, but exclusively to those who were believers themselves.

The Reformers who upheld infant baptism were bitterly at odds with the Anabaptists, and the conflict expressed itself not only in verbal controversy but also in savage persecution. Zwingli had the Anabaptist, Felix Manz, condemned to death by drowning because of the latter's insistence that believers should be immersed ('Let him who talks about going under go under');[39] Luther invoked the civil authorities against Anabaptists;[40] and the controversy about baptism became one of the most divisive issues of the Reformation. Broadly speaking, it was a battle between the concept of Christendom and the notion of a 'gathered', regenerate Church. Among the Anabaptists

> adult baptism came to mean more than a personal act of obedience and loyalty; it became an eloquent way of rejecting Christian sacralism and all it stood for.[41]

The Church of England and the Dissenters

Two main factors, one political, the other theological, brought the Church of England into being. First, Henry VIII, who had earlier been dignified with the title 'Defender of the Faith' in recognition of his opposition to Protestantism, rejected the authority of the Pope. He was content, on the whole, that the Catholic Church in England should remain unaltered in doctrine and liturgy; but it was to have a king,

[38] Ibid., pp.113–19
[39] Ibid., pp.95f.
[40] Ibid., p.106
[41] Ibid.

rather than a bishop, as its head. But second, the theological controversies taking place in Europe excited keen interest in England, as men of learning came into contact with the work of the Reformers. From the beginning, the Church of England was conceived as the religious arm of the nation and infant baptism continued to give practical expression to this belief. The first and second prayer books published during the reign of Edward VI (1549 and 1552) make provision for the baptism of infants only.

It was not long, however, before the European baptismal controversies were reproduced in England. Bridge and Phypers provide us with an admirable account of the circumstances that obtained early in the seventeenth century:

> Church of England was the religion of the realm, by law established. The Church occupied a position definitely Protestant in doctrine, but in many ways Catholic in structure and practice. Every citizen was legally required to be baptized as an infant, to be confirmed as an adult and to attend public worship at an Anglican church. It was the perfect example of the 'sacralist society'.
>
> Within the ranks of Anglicanism were growing numbers of 'Puritans' who wished to retain a state church but were dissatisfied with its current condition, and bent on transforming it from within. Looking to Calvin's Geneva as their ideal, they aimed for a Calvinistic system of doctrine and a presbyterian system of church government. Outside its ranks were the Dissenters or Separatists. They (on the whole) accepted Geneva's doctrine, but believed that it contradicted Geneva's practice. To them a pure and scriptural Church must of necessity have a regenerate membership, and this meant the end of a state church. They gathered groups of Christians on the basis of a personal confession of faith, and regarded them and their children alone as members of the true Church. They became the Independents or Congregationalists of later denominational life. In turn some of them took the logic further: 'Surely', they said, 'regenerate membership leads to the baptism of believers only, and the rebaptism of those merely christened as infants.' Some were influenced by the Dutch Mennonites and, discarding their Calvinistic theology, became 'General Baptists'. Others (the majority) preserved the theology of Geneva and became 'Particular Baptists'.[42]

[42] Ibid., pp. 126f.

It is not part of our purpose in this book to discuss the ways in which the Dissenting denominations in England came into being; but it is relevant to note that, within a hundred years of the break with Rome, the Church of England was itself torn apart by disputes which included disagreements about baptism. The Articles of Religion of the Church of England, first drawn up in 1562, declared that:

> The baptism of young children is in any wise to be retained in the Church, as most agreeable with the institution of Christ.[43]

The Presbyterian wing of the English Church, not yet separated from the parent body, and at this time enjoying its period of greatest influence, declared in 1643 that:

> Not only those that do actually profess faith and obedience unto Christ, but also the infants of one or both believing parents, are to be baptized.[44]

The Independents also administered baptism to the children of their own members, but the Baptists, in a confession of faith drawn up by seven congregations in London in 1646, asserted that:

> Baptism is an ordinance of the New Testament, given by Christ, to be dispensed upon persons *professing faith,* or that are made disciples . . . The way of dispensing this ordinance, is *dipping or plunging the body under water.*[45]

The positions encapsulated in these quotations continue to be held to this day. The Church of England and the United Reformed Church (a union of Presbyterians and Congregationalists) practise paedobaptism; but Baptists churches still maintain that only believers should be baptized.

Methodism
Whether or not it is true that 'every Methodist minister has his

[43] Article 27 of the Church of England
[44] *The Westminster Confession,* Article 28
[45] Quoted in Henry Bettenson, *Documents of the Christian Church,* Second Edition, Oxford University Press, 1967, p.249. This statement was approved by more than one hundred Baptist congregations in 1689

own view of what baptism means',[46] there can be no doubt that official Methodist practice from the time of Wesley to the present day has been paedobaptist. After pointing out that Wesley normally used the 1662 Prayer Book service for the baptism of infants, Trevor Dearing adds:

> In his ministry at Georgia, there is no doubt that Wesley emphasized also the various rites and ceremonies that had appeared in the first Edwardian Prayer Book (1549) and that these were also counted as significant by the Non-Jurors. He baptized by total immersion and signed each child on the forehead with the 'Sign of the Cross'. So strong were his views that he declined to bury any who had not received baptism by an episcopally ordained priest. He also refused the Lord's Supper to persons who were likewise, to him, not properly baptized. He baptized again the children of Dissenters.[47]

According to Rupert E. Davies:

> ... there is no doubt at all that Wesley believed in the baptismal regeneration of infants . . . Lest we be tempted to think that Wesley did not hold this view very wholeheartedly himself, but felt himself forced to accept it on the authority of the Church, he sets out the full arguments for infant baptism as a means of regeneration, the washing away of original sin, admission into the New Covenant and into the Church, and inheritance of the Kingdom of Heaven, in a treatise published specifically for that purpose in 1756, and never retracted. Here he shows that, according to the intention of Jesus, there is no other means of entering the Church, or heaven, and the outward baptism is a necessary means to the inward. He argues that since infants are capable of entering into a covenant; since the infants of believers are included within the covenant of grace; since infants ought to come to Christ and enter his Church; since the Apostles baptized infants; therefore infants are proper subjects for baptism.[48]

Davies raises, and is able to answer, the question of whether Wesley's belief in baptismal regeneration is inconsistent with his other emphases:

[46] Bridge and Phypers, op. cit., p.142

[47] Trevor Dearing, *Wesleyan and Tractarian Worship,* Epworth Press/S.P.C.K., 1966, p.109

[48] *A History of the Methodist Church in Great Britain*, Volume 1, edited by Rupert E. Davies and E. Gordon Rupp, Epworth Press, 1965, p.160

The whole tendency of the rest of Wesley's theology and method seem to go against the doctrine. Faith and repentance are laid down by him time and again as the pre-requisites of the new birth, and he does not try to claim that they are really present in infants ... Yet there is no actual contradiction. He believed that a child once baptized was cleansed from original sin, and if he did not commit actual sin would go to heaven. But every child who remained alive did commit actual sin and needed to be born again for the second time (he said that up to the age of ten years he did not think that he had sinned away the 'washing of the Holy Ghost' given in baptism).[49]

Thus, while he discouraged his hearers from 'relying on that broken reed, that ye *were* born again in baptism,[50] and insisted upon the need for conversion, Wesley did not under-value baptism:

Who denies that ye were then made children of God, and heirs of the Kingdom of Heaven? But notwithstanding this, ye are now children of the devil. Therefore, ye must be born again.[51]

Wesley's high regard for infant baptism seems to have' remained constant throughout his life and the practice has remained normative in Methodism ever since. The Deed of Union (1932) states that:

according to Methodist usage the sacrament of baptism is administered to infants. . .[52]

and as recently as 1975 it was decreed by the Methodist Conference that 'Methodist ministers must be willing to baptize infants in appropriate circumstances'.[53]

This chapter has attempted a sketch of the way in which the practice of infant baptism has developed since apostolic times. Clearly, there is much more to be said about the practice of nineteen hundred years than is possible in such

[49] Ibid., p.161
[50] John Wesley, *Sermons on Several Occasions,* Epworth Press, 1944 edition, p.173
[51] Ibid. p.173
[52] The Deed of Union, Clause 330
[53] Methodist Conference *Minutes,* 1975, p.49

little space, but the main landmarks have been noted. We have seen that the Church's practice is uncertain during the first two centuries; that infant baptism is indisputably prevalent from the year 200 onwards; that by the fourth century it was becoming the norm (in practice, if not theologically); and that it has remained the norm ever since. We have observed the determination of most of the Reformers to retain paedobaptism, although some preferred believers' baptism, and the commitment of the English churches, with few exceptions, to paedobaptism.

Before turning to an examination of the theological arguments for and against infant baptism, we must briefly discuss one other question. *Which* infants were baptized during the centuries we have been considering? Before Constantine, as we have seen, baptism was confined to the children of practising Christians, for the Church was a 'gathered' community, a minority in a hostile or at best indifferent empire. After Constantine, the doctrine of 'sacralism', which intimately links Church and state, led to the view that, in a Christian country, every citizen is a Christian, and to the practice of universal infant baptism throughout Christendom. In established churches this continued after the Reformation; thus, historically, it has been supposed that every Englishman was automatically a member of the Church of England, unless he opted out of it into one of the Dissenting denominations, and therefore the majority of Englishmen have been baptized as infants in the Church of England. Other paedobaptist churches in England, for the greater part of their history, have tended to be gathered churches, and have therefore baptized mainly the offspring of their own members. It should be noted, however, that, particularly in the present century, Free Churches have often provided 'folk religion' in areas where their cultural impact has been as strong as, or stronger than, that of the parish church, and in the process they have baptized children whose parents' allegiance to the Church has been merely nominal.

CHAPTER THREE

The Justification
for Infant Baptism

ALTHOUGH the majority of Christian churches have practised paedobaptism, there has been a sizeable minority of denominations (referred to hereafter as baptists, although this term must be understood to refer not just to the Baptist denomination but to all who practise believers' baptism) who insist on the baptism of believers only. Those who argue the case from either the baptist or the paedobaptist position usually start from the New Testament, attempting to show how the practice of the early Church vindicates their own opinion. But, as we have seen, the New Testament evidence is ambiguous; we cannot assert with any certainty either that the apostolic Church baptized infants or that it did not. The issue, then, cannot be decided on historical evidence, and we must turn to theology for an answer.[1]

New Testament *practice* is uncertain; but it seems proper to ask whether infant baptism is compatible with New Testament *theology*. Both advocates and opponents of infant baptism have addressed themselves to this question, and it is not surprising to learn that they have reached opposite conclusions. The baptist argues that every unambiguous case of baptism recorded in the New Testament is of a person who has been converted to Christ and who consciously believes in him, and maintains that New Testament theology presupposes these circumstances. The paedobaptist, on the other hand, asserts that New Testament doctrine does not preclude infant baptism; indeed he may go further, and argue that the

[1] For the view that, even if the New Testament evidence were not ambiguous, theological and sociological considerations would still have to be weighed against it, see above, pp.33f.

doctrine is better safeguarded by paedobaptism than by believers' baptism. Some paedobaptists, it is true, hold that, since the baptism of adult converts was normative in the early Church, 'New Testament statements about baptism cannot all be used in reference to infant baptism *without modification*'.[2] If those who hold this view are suggesting that the necessary modifications are so momentous that, in effect, a different sacramental theology and therefore a different sacrament from that outlined in the New Testament must emerge, they are deservedly pilloried by baptists. But this is not in fact the case. Arndt, for example, though he refers to the need for modification, makes clear his conviction that

> to think of infant baptism as a different sacrament from believers' baptism would obscure the inseparability of the power of God for salvation and faith.[3]

If the theological defence of infant baptism is to be faithful to the New Testament, the modifications clearly must not be such as to distort the New Testament doctrine. On the other hand, we do well to bear in mind the warnings of Flemington and Arndt. When the baptism of adult converts was the norm in practice, it was also inevitably found to influence the way in which baptismal theology was expressed. A different practice requires some modification of the theology, to take account of the fact that it is infants rather than adults who are being baptized, but not necessarily a significantly different theology. The theology of baptism requires translation rather than re-creation.

Before we turn to the question of whether or not infant baptism is consistent with New Testament theology, one issue remains to be clarified. The paedobaptist is not opposed to believers' baptism in the right circumstances. No one, be he paedobaptist or baptist, is in any doubt that the baptism of adult converts is clearly described in the New Testament, and that the baptism of such people as believers is in every way acceptable. It is indeed inevitable. The paedobaptist

---

[2] Flemington, op.cit., p.135. See also Elmer J. F. Arndt, *The Font and the Table*, Lutterworth Press, 1967, p.51
[3] Ibid., p.54

churches, therefore, practise believers' baptism in strictly missionary situations when adults respond for the first time to the gospel. There is no difference of opinion about this practice between baptists and paedobaptists. But baptists go further, and deny baptism to the children of Christian parents, on the grounds that until a person can come consciously to faith, whether his awareness of Christianity during infancy and childhood has been considerable or negligible, he is ineligible for baptism. Paedobaptists would argue that there is a most significant difference between a person whose background is pagan and one who has been nurtured in a Christian environment, and that the baptism of adults as believers, pre-supposed in a missionary situation, is not applicable to a situation in which the Christian upbringing of children can reasonably be expected. The baptism of converts from outside Christianity is attested in the New Testament and needs no further theological justification. But neither the paedobaptist practice of baptizing infants nor the baptist practice of withholding baptism from infants has unassailable warrant in the practice of the early Church; both, therefore, must come under the scrutiny of New Testament theology.

At the end of Chapter One, we summarized the New Testament theology of baptism in seven clauses. It is now our intention to discuss how consistent infant baptism is with each of them.

1. *The grace of God and his mighty acts of redemption in the life, death and resurrection of Jesus Christ provide the context from which Christian baptism takes its meaning, and alone make it possible.*

> The practice of infant baptism is in itself an impressive witness to the truth that the grace of God comes before our response, and is wholly apart from our deserts.[4]

Paedobaptists often adduce the argument that infant baptism is a better witness than believers' baptism to the prevenient grace of God. This is a strong argument; it rests upon the New Testament doctrine that God is the prime mover in mankind's

---

[4] Methodist Conference Statement on Holy Baptism, *Minutes*, 1952, p.228

salvation. 'You did not choose me; I chose you.'[5] The priority
of God's grace must certainly be safeguarded in any doctrine
and practice of baptism. As the Faith and Order Commission
of the World Council of Churches puts it:

> When his Church at his command baptizes men, it is in reality
> Christ himself who baptizes. Baptism is not merely a human act,
> either of the one who administers or the one who receives it, but it
> is divine . . . Baptism is a work of God, his mighty work, not a
> work of ours. Baptism is the gracious dealing of the Triune God
> with us, 'not because of deeds done by us in righteousness, but in
> virtue of his own mercy, by the washing of regeneration and
> renewal in the Holy Spirit' (Tit. 3:5), and is therefore
> administered in the name of the Trinity. We *are* baptized—it is
> something that is done to us, not something which we ourselves
> do.[6]

Every denomination which practises baptism would assent to
that statement. The validity and effectiveness of baptism are
wholly dependent upon the grace of God. Salvation cannot be
earned or deserved; it is God's free gift;[7] and baptism is, at the
very least, a proclamation of that truth. The paedobaptist,
however, differs from the baptist in believing that infant
baptism does justice to the priority of divine grace in a way
that believers' baptism cannot. Thus Flemington writes:

> Infant baptism, so far from being less evangelical than believers'
> baptism, is in reality more so, because it even more unmistakably
> embodies the primary truth of the Christian gospel, namely that
> the grace of God comes before everything else, and that man's
> only hope of salvation rests upon that Act of God in Jesus Christ,
> from which (as the chief writers of the New Testament so clearly
> and so unanimously demonstrate) this sacrament of the gospel
> draws all its meaning and efficacy.[8]

But in what way does infant baptism more effectively demonstrate God's prevenient grace? Bridge and Phypers summarize the paedobaptist argument:

[5] John 15:16
[6] *One Lord, One Baptism*, S.C.M. Press, 1960, pp.56f.
[7] Ephesians 2:8ff; 1 John 4:19
[8] Flemington, op. cit., pp.146f.

Because salvation is objective, the reasoning goes, adult baptism tends to emphasize the subjective response of the convert rather than the objective fact of God's grace. Paedobaptism, on the other hand, by being performed on those who cannot exercise conscious faith, more aptly portrays the objective nature of salvation and the necessity for the sovereignty of God in its execution.[9]

On this view, infant baptism is a splendid proclamation of the sovereign, prevenient grace of God, because it is administered to one who, in the nature of things, cannot claim anything for himself. The infant cannot request baptism, nor can he profess faith; he is entirely dependent upon others. In particular, he is dependent upon God's grace. Baptist practice, however, cannot clearly demonstrate belief in the priority of grace, because it requires the believer's faith as a precondition of baptism.

Baptist scholars, of course, do not accept this assessment of the two practices. Thus R. E. O. White takes up the point at issue:

Unguarded emphasis upon the prevenience of grace tends to represent the divine will as entirely arbitrary, an idea against which the whole biblical revelation consistently protests. Arbitrariness is suggested whenever it is argued that 'God does not consult man when he creates him . . . Infants are no more responsible for being baptized than they are for being created.' If indeed God can, in sovereign, prevenient, arbitrary grace, baptize some into salvation, whose fault is it that the whole world is not saved? . . .The other side of this danger is that of misreading entirely the nature of grace. Forsyth's warning against 'the materialization of grace' is still necessary, and Baillie echoes it: 'grace is not a transferable substance but a living personal relationship'. When this is truly evaluated, much of the talk about the 'operation' of grace upon the 'helpless' infant, 'incapable of exercising faith' and 'having not yet any self-conscious existence at all', loses its meaning. Grace must not be divorced, by an exaggerated doctrine of prevenience, from religious reality, or from the preaching of the gospel.[10]

Few paedobaptists would deny that there is some force in

[9] Bridge and Phypers, op. cit., p.40
[10] R. E. O. White, op. cit., pp.283f.

White's argument. He is surely right to insist that, as Arndt puts it, 'there are two "sides" to baptism: (1) the divine action; and (2) the response of the baptized'.[11] Although some theologians have argued that baptism is efficacious *ex opere operato,* most paedobaptists would shrink from this mechanical view. If baptism is effective solely by virtue of its administration, those Jesuits in North America who furtively sprinkled every baby in sight while they muttered the formula of conditional baptism[12] were entirely justified; and the Church should be committed to a policy of totally indiscriminate baptism.

But the rejection of an *ex opere operato* doctrine of baptism and the recognition that baptism involves both divine action and human response do not add up to a refutation of the paedobaptist argument about the priority of God's grace. For the paedobaptist who asserts that infant baptism more effectively proclaims the prevenience and sovereignty of divine grace does not deny the need for a response on the part of the baptized. Apart from those who cling to *ex opere operato* opinions, paedobaptists accept that both the divine action and the human response are important. The crucial question, therefore, is whether the human response to grace must necessarily *precede* baptism, as the baptist holds, or can validly *follow* baptism. In the next section of this chapter, we shall examine the relationship between faith and baptism. At present, it will be sufficient for us to note that the paedobaptist does not rule out the need for a human response; but he does maintain that God's grace is not in any way dependent upon man's merit, or understanding, or faith, that it is prevenient and sovereign, and that infant baptism is an eloquent testimony to that belief.

2. *Baptism is inseparably linked with faith. The New Testament has nothing to say about baptism without faith or faith without baptism.*

At no point, perhaps, is the divergence between the general pattern of New Testament teaching and the practice of infant

[11] Arndt, op. cit., pp.44f.
[12] See the article by A. R. Vidler in *Theology,* July 1940, p.4

baptism more keenly felt than at the point of the intimate relation between faith and baptism. The evidence of the Acts of the Apostles is unmistakable. Baptism follows acceptance of the message: it is 'heard' or 'received' or 'believed'. To receive baptism is to give expression to one's faith: by being baptized, a person appropriated to himself the meaning of the gospel. And this is not possible for the infant.[13]

If the paedobaptist can claim that infant baptism more effectively testifies to the prevenient grace of God, the baptist is at his strongest when he discusses the relationship between baptism and faith. Every indisputable account of the practice of baptism in the New Testament suggests that baptism was administered to a professing believer on the basis of his faith. From this the baptist concludes that paedobaptism is indefensible: because the infant cannot be said to have faith, he is unable to meet the pre-condition of baptism. Both the divine action and the human response must be present if baptism is to retain its New Testament meaning.

The paedobaptist accepts the relationship, in New Testament practice, between faith and baptism, and, as we have already noted, agrees that the model of believers' baptism is entirely appropriate for converted pagans. He is not prepared to press the argument from the priority of God's grace to its logical but absurd conclusion—the indiscriminate baptism of every human being. But the paedobaptist, while admitting the need for a human response of faith, is by no means convinced that the baptist has hit upon the only way of relating baptism with faith, or the best, in circumstances other than those of a strictly missionary nature. How then does the paedobaptist see the relationship between faith and baptism?

One attempt to describe the relationship has been made by those, including Martin Luther,[14] who have endeavoured to show that infant faith is actually possible. But most paedobaptists have eschewed such attempts to suggest that babies can have personal faith, preferring to make frank acknowledgement of the absence of faith on the part of the recipients of

[13] Arndt, op. cit., p.51
[14] See Bridge and Phypers, op. cit., p.52

infant baptism, and looking elsewhere for the link between baptism and faith.

Many paedobaptists find the connection in the concept of vicarious faith. The New Testament provides several accounts of miraculous cures which occurred when the faith, not of the individuals cured, but of others was operative. Divine action and human faith are both involved, but the faith is vicarious. Thus Jairus' daughter,[15] the centurion's servant,[16] a paralytic,[17] and an epileptic boy[18] were all healed in the context of faith, though the faith was not their own. None of these stories, of course, is in any way concerned with baptism; but paedobaptists find in them a basis for the belief that one man's faith may avail for another. Thus, though an infant cannot be said to have faith, the faith necessary for baptism may be supplied by his parents, or his godparents, or the Church. As Flemington writes:

> The fact that an infant cannot exercise faith does not mean that in infant baptism there is no place for faith. On the contrary, there is no occasion when faith is more necessary; but the faith is that of the worshipping Church and of Christian parents—the faith of the Church, which knows that it is the Body of Christ, and that it has the power in his name to 'receive this child into the congregation of Christ's flock', and the faith of parents, whose care it is to bring up their children 'in the fear and nurture of the Lord and to the praise of his holy name'.[19]

Flemington is surely right to mention the faith of both Church and parents. Baptism is a sacrament of the Church; it signifies entry into the Church; [20] it is therefore important that the Church should exercise faith on behalf of the children whom it baptizes. But the faith of parents is also important. Those who exercised faith on behalf of the paralytic, the epileptic and the rest were close relatives or friends. If vicarious faith is to be exercised on behalf of a child, part of that faith should surely be that of his closest relatives.

[15] Matthew 9:18, 23–26
[16] Matthew 8:5–13
[17] Matthew 9:1f.
[18] Matthew 17:14–21
[19] Flemington, op.cit., pp.144f.
[20] See below, pp.65f.

There is yet another way in which the relationship between baptism and faith can be understood. Baptism may be seen as an anticipation of faith:

> The practice of infant baptism occurs in a context in which stress is laid upon corporate faith, upon an environment of faith, rather than upon the explicit decision of the recipient of baptism. Here the whole community affirms its faith in God and pledges itself to provide such an environment of faith, in the home, and in the worship, instruction and witness of the Church. The necessity of (sic) the baptized himself to believe is in no way diminished, far less removed. The claim and promise of the gospel are laid on the child in baptism to which a response must be owned and which must be received by faith if the fruits of baptism are to be known and to flourish in his life. Thus in the baptism of infants, the rite does not take the place of faith, but demands it.[21]

If the baptist maintains that infant baptism is baptism without faith, the paedobapist may reply, not only that faith is present—vicarious faith, exercised on the child's behalf by the Church and by parents—but also that paedobaptism looks forward to the day when the baptized will consciously profess faith. Faith and baptism belong together, but need not occur in that chronological order.

The idea that baptism can justifiably anticipate faith is expressed in a Methodist Conference Memorandum of 1936:

> The outward act anticipates the day when the child will consciously accept the inward grace. Our hope and confidence is that, through the operation of the Holy Spirit, in answer to the prayers of the Church, and through the influence of the Christian nurture to which the parents pledge themselves, this sacrament will be inwardly completed and made effective when the child through faith in Christ responds to the grace proclaimed and pledged by the rite.[22]

It is also important to recognize that post-baptismal faith is required of all the baptized, at whatever age the individual receives baptism. Faith before baptism, in the case of a con-

[21] *One Lord, One Baptism,* pp.63f.
[22] Methodist Conference *Minutes,* 1936, p.400

vert, is not the only faith that counts in relation to his baptism: for after baptism he is to live the life of faith, progressively 'becoming what he is'. Baptism is a beginning; its benefits continue to be appropriated by faith.

The baptist finds the paedobaptist's rationale of the link between baptism and faith unacceptable; he argues that the only relevant faith is that of the baptized, and that this faith must be demonstrated before baptism. But the paedobaptist is in a position, not merely to defend infant baptism on the grounds so far suggested, but also to point out a flaw in the baptist's own case.

Colin Buchanan[23] has recently drawn attention to the fact that, in New Testament times, there was no catechumenate. Baptism was administered to converts *immediately* after their profession of faith. But this is not how baptists today generally practise believers' baptism. Even with adults, there tends to be a period of probation and testing, during which the Church seeks to be certain of the genuineness of the candidates' faith. As far as children are concerned, the baptist seems to be incapable of accepting that children can have faith (Buchanan suggests that this is in fact possible from quite an early age)[24] and defers baptism until *in his opinion* the candidates' faith can be adjudged genuine. Thus, if Buchanan is correct, a child who first exercises personal faith at the age of five or six years may have to wait for nine or ten years before he can be baptized.

> The bearing of all this on infant baptism should be obvious. The question is 'At what age is the child of a Christian home *first* entitled to be treated as a Christian?' Whatever the answer to that question may be, it is at *that* age that he or she must be baptized. Any delay beyond that first point involves a subtle change in the role of baptism. It ceases to be an initiation and becomes a witness or reward. And it does not have those roles in the New Testament.[25]

There is a good deal of force in Buchanan's argument. The

---

[23] Colin O. Buchanan, *A Case for Infant Baptism*, Grove Booklets, 1973, pp.15f. (cited hereafter as Buchanan, *A Case*)
[24] Ibid., p.26
[25] Ibid., p.16

absence of a catechumenate in apostolic times shows that
there could have been no certainty about the genuineness of
the faith of many people who received baptism. Even more
important is the point that, if the baptist can fault the
paedobaptist for administering baptism to those who cannot
be said to have faith, he is himself open to censure for denying
baptism to those who *do* profess faith. If a six-year-old child,
who professes faith, asks 'What is to prevent me being baptized?' (Acts 8:36), the baptist will have to search hard for an
answer that will satisfy his own desire to vindicate his practice
from the New Testament.

3. *Baptism is closely associated with the activity of the Holy
Spirit, who came upon Jesus at his baptism, and who is
described as indwelling and sealing those who are baptized.*

In the last section, we referred to the importance of post-
baptismal faith, and insisted that a response to God's grace,
whether or not it has occurred before baptism, certainly ought
to occur after baptism. The Holy Spirit is at work among the
baptized, bringing them to awareness of the things of God and
leading them on to further ventures of faith and discipleship.
No one would deny that those who are baptized as professing
believers can be brought to maturity in this way by the Holy
Spirit; and there seems to be no great difficulty in envisaging
the Spirit's activity within a baptized child.

For if we believe that the Holy Spirit is everywhere at work,
there can be no doubt that he is at work in the baptized child
(or indeed in the unbaptized child). Though it is impossible to
estimate the direct influence of the Spirit on the developing
infant, it seems clear that the Christian environment into
which baptism should admit him will provide opportunities
for the influence of the Spirit to be felt. This is not to say that
an unbaptized child of Christian parents, reared in a
thoroughly Christian environment, will not be the recipient of
similar influences; rather it suggests that, if a child is within
the sphere of the Spirit's work, there is every reason to
baptize him.

Moreover, if we are correct in asserting that the baptized
should come to understand that Christ's redeeming work

applies to him and should respond to Christ in gratitude, faith and obedience, we are surely also right in thinking that the influence of the Spirit will be geared towards these ends. Through the example and instruction offered by Christian parents and through the worship and fellowship of the Church, the Spirit testifies to the baptized that he is God's child,[26] and helps him to grow into what baptism proclaims him to be.

These considerations about the work of the Spirit do not, by themselves, help either to prove or to disprove the paedobaptist case. But, taken together with what we have said above about growing and developing faith and with what we shall say below, in section 7, about the place of children within the Christian family, they suggest that infant baptism is justifiable.

4. *Baptism is a means of cleansing. Unlike Jewish purification ceremonies, it is not repeated, but symbolizes once and for all the cleansing from sin which is available, as a result of Christ's work, to those who are 'in Christ'.*

As we indicated in Chapter One, the notion of cleansing is a dominant motif in New Testament baptismal theology. A man goes into the water dirty; he comes out clean. Baptists, whether they use flowing rivers or baptistries indoors, retain in their rite of total immersion a very compelling dramatic setting for baptism, which effectively illustrates the truth that baptism is a cleansing rite. It is undeniable that a few drops of water sprinkled on a baby's head are a much less impressive witness to this truth. But the concept of baptismal cleansing raises a far more important question for paedobaptism than that of effective symbolism.

Baptism, the argument goes, is concerned with cleansing, with the removal of sin. But in what sense can an infant, perhaps only a few days or even hours old, be said to be sinful? He has had no opportunity to commit sin. How then can baptism, which is concerned with the washing away of sin, be applied to infants?

We cannot dodge this question, as some paedobaptists do,

[26] Romans 8:16

or admit that notions of cleansing and forgiveness do not apply to infants, for we have argued that infant baptism, if it is to be vindicated, must be vindicated by reference to New Testament theology. If the concept of cleansing cannot be applied to infant baptism, infant baptism fails to measure up to New Testament theology, where the concept supplies one of the fundamental meanings of baptism.

At least since Augustine, however, paedobaptists have used the doctrine of original sin to explain how infant baptism can be understood as a washing away of sin. Augustine seems to have argued from infant baptism to the doctrine of original sin, but there is no reason why the process should not be reversed. Original sin is, of course, to be distinguished from actual sin. The capacity to act in a certain way is not the same thing as the act. A man may be pre-disposed to idleness and yet be industrious. There is no dispute about the proposition that a newborn child has committed no actual sin. But what makes us so sure that that is true? It is the fact that he has been in the world for so short a time, that he has not yet had opportunity to assert himself against others or to give way to rage or jealousy or malice that convinces us. We do not, on the whole, argue that there is an innate innocence in the newborn child, though we have no hesitation in believing him innocent of actual sin. It is the opportunity to sin that is lacking. We could, of course, speculate on the possibility that, when the opportunity to sin is presented to him, he may reject it and grow up sinless; but that would be like arguing that the sun may not rise tomorrow. It is logically possible that the sun will not rise tomorrow, but all our observations and the inherited knowledge upon which we depend in order to organize our lives require us to believe that it will. The probability that the familiar pattern will repeat itself yet again is so great that we treat the sun's rising as a certainty. Similarly, our observations of humanity suggest to us that all human beings are capable of sin and that, once they have the opportunity to commit sin, they do so. This is where the doctrine of original sin comes into play. Far from asserting that every human being is born innocent but then falls prey to sin by committing actual sins, this doctrine maintains that each person brings a sinful nature into the world with him. He is born with a predisposition towards sin; and this is just as much an inherited characteristic as are such genetically controlled features of a child as the colour of his eyes.

There is no need to base this argument on the alleged historicity of the myth of Adam and Eve,[27] though this story is a picturesque description of 'the way things are'.[28] Nor is it necessary to believe that babies, being guilty from birth, are consigned to hell if they die unbaptized. Such a concept is alien to modern thought and, for that matter, is not compatible with the scriptures, 'which nowhere suggest that, when we are born, we are already guilty, already responsible and punishable for Sin or sins'.[29] Without leading us to such lengths, however, the doctrine of original sin has an important bearing on infant baptism. For a baby who cannot be said to have committed any actual sin which needs washing away *can* be said to have inherited the burden of original sin. Though we may not accept that the baby individually needs to be forgiven, we recognize that he takes his place in a sinful humanity, sharing with all his fellow human beings a predisposition towards sin. Humanity's sin needs forgiveness; and that portion of it that attaches itself to the child, though he is not responsible for it, needs forgiveness too. Thus the concept of baptismal cleansing is not inappropriate: a child may have a dirty face as a result of another person's negligence or incompetence or stupidity, but his face still requires washing.

It must be admitted that not every paedobaptist would subscribe to the case we have presented. Quick, for example, although he believes in original sin, declares that 'this whole account of the matter is open to grave objection':[30]

What cannot at all be verified in experience is the supposition that baptism in itself makes any such change in the spiritual condition of an infant as is implied by asserting that it removes from it once and for all original sin and its hold on the soul. So far as experience can show, the sinful tendencies or spiritual defects

[27] Genesis 3
[28] John Stacey, *Groundwork of Theology*, Epworth Press, 1977, p.257
[29] Rupert E. Davies in *An Approach to Christian Doctrine*, edited by Greville P. Lewis, Epworth Press, 1954, p.61
[30] Oliver Chase Quick, *The Christian Sacraments*, Nisbet & Co., 1927, p.172

of a baptized and of an unbaptized child are very much the same.[31]

Flemington, who shares Quick's hesitations, suggests that:

It would seem more in accord both with the facts of moral experience and with the teaching of the New Testament to describe the relation between baptism and sin by seeing in the rite as administered to infants the divine pledge and promise, for a particular life, that all sin (whether original sin or actual sin) shall ultimately be overcome, because Christ overcame it once for all in the victory of the Cross.[32]

Flemington's explanation may seem to be an evasion; he sees baptism as a proleptic sign of forgiveness and victory rather than as an actual means of cleansing. But there is clearly some force in his claim that, whatever else it is, baptism is a pledge of future victory over sin. We need not opt, however, for either our own previous suggestion that infant baptism means the washing away of original sin or Flemington's explanation, for these are false alternatives, introduced into the discussion by a basic misunderstanding.

Quick makes the mistake of expecting to see a difference between the moral and spiritual characteristics of baptized and unbaptized children if indeed baptism cleanses from original sin. But this expectation is unreasonable, in that it takes no account of the existence of post-baptismal sin *at whatever age* baptism is administered. The Corinthians were baptized; so were the Colossians; but Paul finds it necessary to appeal to them to live up to the meaning of their baptism.[33] Paul was well aware of the fact that sin was committed after baptism, deplorable as this may be. For a short time in the long history of the Church, it was widely held that post-baptismal sin was unforgivable—a doctrine which led to widespread postponements of baptism.[34] But the general wisdom of the Church has been to acknowledge that, although baptism means a new beginning, the old life continues to break in from time to time.

[31] Ibid.
[32] Flemington, op. cit., p.140
[33] See 1 Corinthians 6:9ff.; Colossians 2:20, 3:1–5
[34] See above, pp.36f.

Thus orthodoxy has acknowledged the continuing existence of sin among the baptized and the continuing need for forgiveness. Thus the eucharist contains penitential prayers and a substantial number of Christians value the confessional. If the existence of post-baptismal sin is an argument against seeing infant baptism as an act of cleansing, it is also an argument against seeing any sort of baptism in this way.

But no baptist would claim that, once he has been baptized, he is free from sin. He will wish to persevere in faith, becoming what he is, as will the baptized child who learns to take his baptism seriously. But he will scarcely dare to suggest that baptism has dealt conclusively with sin in such a way that he will never again commit it. It is not necessary to believe that there is no post-baptismal sin in order to believe that baptism is a rite of cleansing.

It seems sensible to conclude, therefore, that baptism, whether administered to infants or to adults, is a means whereby all sin, original or actual, which *at that point in time* attaches itself to the recipient is forgiven. But this is not all. For, as Flemington correctly maintains, baptism is *also* a declaration that all subsequent sin can find forgiveness as the individual responds to God's grace in penitence and faith. Since baptism looks forward in this way to an ultimate victory over sin, it is neither necessary nor possible for baptism to be repeated.

We have attempted to show that the doctrine of baptismal cleansing can apply to infants as well as to believers. But there is a further point to be made. Just as infant baptism can be described as a better demonstration of the prevenient grace of God than believers' baptism, it is also a more powerful symbol of God's power and will to overcome sin. Before an infant has had opportunity to commit actual sin, God's grace and forgiveness are available to him.

5. *Baptism is a new beginning. This may be described as a rebirth, or as a sharing in Christ's death and resurrection. The powerful symbol of entering the water, being immersed in it, and emerging from it represents not merely a change of status but also a change of life-style. Thus the great Pauline doctrines*

of justification and sanctification, both closely associated with faith, are also closely related to baptism.

Much controversy has centred on the doctrine of baptismal regeneration. We have seen that the doctrine has a strong biblical basis.[35] It is emphasized in *The Book of Common Prayer* (1662), which states that 'baptism is a sign of regeneration or new birth'[36] and has no hesitation in declaring a baptized child to be regenerate.[37] But some evangelical Anglicans find this concept difficult to accept, and it is said that 'Methodism by and large rejects'[38] it. Once again, however, we must endeavour to show that infant baptism is compatible with New Testament theology, in which regeneration is clearly found—a task to which Flemington addresses himself:

> It is arguable that the concept of regeneration has, among many evangelicals, been given too wide an interpretation, and has been wrongly taken to include spiritual processes which more properly belong to other stages of the Christian life, and can therefore more appropriately be described by the use of other terms. If this language about 'regeneration' and 'divine sonship' be understood to refer to the *first beginnings* of the new life (which God alone can implant within the soul), and to the *new status* of those who are received within the covenant (a status which only God can bestow), then there would seem no good reason why such phrases affirming regeneration should not be used as truly of infant baptism as they were in New Testament times concerning the baptism of adults. . . Moreover, the analogy of physical birth would suggest a certain appropriateness in the use of this language in reference to the baptism of infants. Just as in the natural order we are 'born in another's pain', so, too, in the spiritual order we have 'life by his death'—and each of these antedates our own knowledge and consciousness of the fact.[39]

By placing the emphasis firmly upon the divine act of begetting and the fact that baptism means the *beginning* of a new

[35] See above, pp.21f.
[36] Article 27
[37] 'Publick Baptism of Infants'
[38] John Stacey, op. cit., p.335
[39] Flemington, op. cit., p.141

life, Flemington shows that infant baptism can justifiably be described as an act of regeneration. As for the great Pauline concept of dying and rising with Christ, of which the total immersion practised by baptists is admittedly a more powerful dramatic symbol, this must be thought of as a proleptic sign of what is to come. The baptized child must learn what it means to die with Christ and to rise with him, just as a child born into the world must learn to speak and to walk. He is born into an environment in which such things are possible.

It may be argued that, if we profess to believe that infant baptism is an act of regeneration and of participation in Christ's death and resurrection, we ought to be able to say more than is said in the previous paragraph. But first, we would maintain that no more than that can be said of believers' baptism. Baptism means participation in Christ's death and resurrection, but the rite itself, although it symbolically sums up the whole process, is essentially the beginning of the process. The believer will soon discover that dying and rising is something which has to be repeated existentially again and again. Second, we would point out that Paul sees fit to encourage the Colossians to 'put to death' that which belongs to the lower nature[40] and exhorts the Romans to live as those who have died to sin.[41] Exhortations such as these would be meaningless if Paul had considered baptism to be complete in itself.

The new beginning which baptism provides places the baptized in a position where he must, as we have repeatedly stated, learn to become what he is. That is as true of believers as it is of infants. But once again, infant baptism may be thought to indicate more clearly that we are reborn as a result of the divine initiative. We do not bring ourselves to birth.

6. *Baptism signifies that a person belongs to God (as did circumcision in the Old Covenant) and that he is included in God's kingdom, now and in the future.*

The story of Jesus rebuking his disciples for trying to turn children away from him (Mark 10:13–16) is included in many

[40] Colossians 3:1–17
[41] Romans 6:1–14

liturgies of infant baptism, despite the fact that it is apparently not directly concerned with baptism. Some paedobaptists argue that, because the story indicates that Jesus accepted children gladly and taught that the kingdom of heaven belonged to such as these, it lends support to the practice of infant baptism. Others, indeed, would go further:

> Cullmann has collected sufficient evidence to suggest that the phrase 'forbid them not' is a deliberate allusion to the baptismal rite of the early Church, where the question 'what hinders?' was asked liturgically before the candidates were baptized (cf. esp. Acts 8:38, 10:47 . . .). The concluding verse of the pericope (10:16), 'he took them in his arms and blessed them, laying his hands upon them', is, of course, the literal description of the minister's action at the baptism of infants, then as now.[42]

This suggestion is attractive and by no means far-fetched; but it remains speculative. In discussing the view that baptism, as a sign that a person belongs to God, can justifiably be applied to infants, we are perhaps on firmer ground when we turn to covenant theology.

Paedobaptists who invoke covenant theology in support of infant baptism maintain that there is continuity rather than discontinuity between the Old Testament (or covenant) and the New. The nation of Israel becomes the Church, the 'Israel of God';[43] circumcision gives way to baptism;[44] the eucharist assumes the place of the passover.[45] But there is no change in the basis of the covenant: God's initiative of grace, nor in the fact that God has a covenant people.[46] The significance of this for baptism is that the Old Testament specifically includes children in the covenant, for example, with Noah and with Abraham.[47] It is not surprising, therefore, that when we turn to the New Testament we should discover that

---

[42] Alan Richardson, *An Introduction to the Theology of the New Testament*, S.C.M. Press, 1958, p.361
[43] Galatians 6:16
[44] Colossians 2:11f.
[45] 1 Corinthians 5:7; 11:25
[46] 1 Peter 2:9f.
[47] Genesis 6:18; 9:8–13; 17:7. See also Psalm 103:17f.; Isaiah 59:20f. Examples could be multiplied

The same principle that God includes children in his covenant dealings with their parents is similarly found. On the Day of Pentecost Peter declared, 'The promise is to you *and to your children*' (Acts 2:39). The angel who appeared to Cornelius promised a message by which he would be saved *and all his household* (Acts 11:14). Paul announced to the Philippian gaoler, 'Believe in the Lord Jesus, and you will be saved, *you and your household*' (Acts 16:31) . . . Children in the churches at Ephesus and Colossae were addressed in the same breath as their parents (Eph. 6:1–3; Col. 3:20). Thus, it is concluded, the covenant of grace is one, the same in both Old and New Testaments. It is a covenant of salvation by faith and also a covenant in which children share its blessings on account of their parents' faith.[48]

This case, which depends upon the assumption that parents presenting their children for baptism are themselves heirs of the covenant, was vigorously argued by Calvin,[49] and has commended itself to many paedobaptists since the Reformation. Its most powerful exponent in recent years has been Marcel:

> By a sovereign decree, independently of any human point of view, God decides that the children of believers shall be included in his covenant.[50]

7. *Like Jewish proselyte baptism, Christian baptism signifies entry into a community. The Church is made up of the baptized. Baptism, as a result, is a mark of the unity of the Church; and there are to be no racial or social distinctions among the baptized.*

'The couple belong to the congregation, so the child belongs to it too.' This is simple social fact; the child grasps this truth, as Calvin puts it, not intellectually but experientially. It is one of the *givens* of his young life. He is sealed in the covenant as surely as his nationality is fixed. Both are in the air he breathes until such time as he breaks the seals or confirms them. This is why we find it hard to concede to the Baptist practice of mere dedication. The child is

---

[48] Bridge and Phypers, op. cit., pp. 46f.

[49] See Peter Chave, in an article in *Epworth Review*, May 1976, pp.74–80

[50] Pierre Ch. Marcel, *The Biblical Doctrine of Infant Baptism*, James Clarke and Company, 1953, p.191

already an heir of the covenant—willy-nilly; 'If they are participants in the thing signified, why shall they be debarred from the
sign?'[51]

Here the baptist is at his weakest. As Chave says, for children
born into a Christian family, belonging to the Church is a
'simple social fact'. By being taken to worship and invited to
join in hymns and prayers, children are being treated as
Christian children. In a pungent chapter, Colin Buchanan[52]
asks baptist parents, 'How will you bring up your own children?', and emphasizes not only that children can believe in
Christ from a very early age but also that it is quite impossible
in practice for parents to treat their children as unbelievers
while involving them in the life of the Church. If children are
to be treated as people who belong to the Church, they ought
to be baptized, for baptism is the means of entry into the
Church. To defer baptism is to suggest that children do not
belong.

In this chapter we have attempted to show that infant
baptism can be vindicated by New Testament theology. All
the New Testament insights into the nature of baptism, we
have suggested, can be applied to infants as well as to believers, and in the context of a Christian upbringing, some of
them even apply with greater force to infants. One theological
consideration, however, remains to be discussed. Which
infants are to be baptized? The practicalities of infant baptism
will engage our attention in Part Two of this book, but we
ought to make clear at this point the implications of our
historical and theological study.

Some of the statements which we have made in defence of
infant baptism might be thought to support the view that
'indiscriminate' baptism is justified. Inasmuch as baptism is a
sign of God's prevenient grace, available to all mankind, it
could be said that every baby (indeed every unbaptized
human being) should be able to receive it. Inasmuch as baptism signifies a washing away of original sin, every child is a
suitable candidate. Inasmuch as Jesus loved and accepted
children, baptism ought to be administered to all children as a

[51] Chave, op.cit., p.77. The last sentence is a quotation from Calvin
[52] Buchanan, *A Case*, pp.25ff.

proclamation of the divine love and of the conviction that the kingdom of heaven belongs to such as these.

Yet the weight of the theological evidence is against 'indiscriminate' baptism. In rejecting *ex opere operato* views of baptism, we asserted the need for faith on the part of those close to the infant, and insisted that opportunities must be presented to all the baptized to become what they are. New birth, we maintained, must lead to new living; the opportunity to learn what it means to die and rise again with Christ must be presented. And in arguing from covenant theology and the doctrine that baptism means incorporation into the Church, we emphasized the role of parents, who are themselves heirs of the covenant and members of the Body.

If we are to be faithful to the total witness of New Testament theology, then, and not just to selected parts of it, we contend that the theological case for infant baptism cannot be applied indiscriminately. Our historical study has already shown this has never been done by the Church.[53] Parents of baptized infants have always been deemed to be Christians. But in the present age, the business of assessing which parents can be described as Christians and which cannot is, as we shall see in Part Two, peculiarly difficult.

Before turning to this pressing practical issue, we must spend some time on other matters. Baptism is not an isolated event; and in particular it must be related to the whole process of initiation, to religious experience, and to the other dominical sacrament, the eucharist. We must, therefore, turn our attention to the relationship between baptism and conversion, confirmation and communion.

[53] See above, p.45

CHAPTER FOUR

Baptism, Conversion, Confirmation, Communion

Conversion

> Conversion means turning, or rather being turned, from sin to God, and thus in the Bible it is very similar to repentance, but it has come to mean that whole change in a man's character and outlook which salvation produces.[1]

EVANGELICAL Christians place great emphasis upon conversion as the decisive event in the individual Christian's experience, whether this is understood as a sudden experience or as a process. Methodism stands within the evangelical tradition and, because this book is written in a Methodist context, it is therefore necessary for us to examine the relationship between baptism and conversion.

Baptists have no difficulty in describing the relationship. Conversion, they say, is that act of turning to God in penitence and faith which marks the true beginning of the Christian life. Baptism is administered to the believer, the convert, as an outward sign of the inward change which has occurred. They point to the numerous New Testament references to the baptism of converts as a vindication of this view, though, as we saw in Chapter Three, their current baptismal practice differs from that of the early Church in that baptism is not administered immediately after the first profession of faith. Paedobaptists would also want to assert the rightness of infant baptism for the children of Christians on some or all of the grounds suggested in the previous chapter. So, on the paedobaptist view, if conversion is to occur in the case of those baptized in infancy, it must obviously *follow* baptism.

[1] A. Raymond George in *An Approach to Christian Doctrine*, p.116

Paedobaptists who use the language of conversion, therefore, see it as the moment in which (or the gradual process through which) the baptized comes to appropriate to himself all that is available to him as a result of his baptism and consciously endorses the actions performed on his behalf. He was baptized because others had faith; now he has faith of his own. He was made a member of the Church long before he could have any say in the matter; now he gladly acknowledges his membership. Conversion, on this view, is the event (sudden or gradual) which makes real to the individual the relationship with God that has always been available to him. It is the individual's response to God's prevenient grace. To use a crude illustration, we might say that the mains water supply is connected up and the household plumbing is in working order. Once the tap has been turned on, the water will flow. The necessary work has been accomplished in baptism; conversion is the turning on of the tap, the individual's act of claiming what is available to him.

> This sacrament (i.e. baptism) will be inwardly complete and made effective when the child through faith in Christ responds to the grace proclaimed and pledged by the rite.[2]

But perhaps 'conversion' is not the best word to describe the event in the case of a child brought up within a Christian family, appropriate though it remains for a person who comes into Christianity from outside. Although 'conversion' is a New Testament word, its occurrences are restricted to people who, in believing in Christ, turned from Judaism or paganism. It is never applied to the children of Christian parents, nurtured in the faith. As we saw in Chapter Three, such parents inevitably bring up their children in the Christian faith and involve them in the life of the believing and worshipping community. The children are treated as Christian children. This is not to deny that it is essential that every baptized person should come to have personal faith; once faith has become a possibility, its existence is vital to the continuing efficacy of baptism. But what we have said does call into question the use of the word 'conversion' in these

---

[2] From the Methodist Conference Memorandum of 1936

cases. Everyone needs a personal relationship with Christ and a commitment to him; but not everyone needs to be converted from another religion or from paganism: some may be said to grow into what they are, to develop in the spiritual life and they develop in other respects, without changing direction in any way.

Conversion, we are suggesting, is a suitable concept to apply to those who make a deliberate decision to become Christians—a decision which involves them in turning from another way of life. If they have not been baptized, baptism will logically follow their conversion. In other cases, where infant baptism has been administered but where insufficient nurture has been provided or where the baptized person has rejected the claims of Christ and then changed course again, conversion is once more a suitable description of what has happened. Here baptism has preceded conversion. But it remains true that some children baptized in infancy may grow up in an environment of Christian love and faith and may find themselves in a personal relationship with Christ, without ever having been converted. They have never held a belief or had a life-style from which they needed to be converted.

This assessment of the relationship between baptism and conversion will not commend itself to those evangelicals who, while recognizing that people's experiences vary in detail, still maintain that everyone without exception needs to be converted. Some years ago, in a meeting of ministers, one of the men present remarked that the Church was having difficulty in these days in 'keeping our own children and converting those from outside'. Another minister immediately objected that his colleague should have said 'converting our own children and those from outside'. But in the end, this is a quibble about words. The essential thing, as we have tried to show, is for each baptized person to have a developing personal faith.

The relationship between baptism and conversion is not merely of academic interest, for it has a bearing on a practical problem which has occurred from the time of the Reformation onwards and which some evangelicals in particular still experience. Not infrequently, a person baptized in infancy, having had a dramatic religious experience, rejects his infant baptism as invalid and requests baptism as a believer. An article in the evangelical magazine, *Crusade,*[3] recently described the experience of Mr Nigel Perrin, a member of the renowned vocal ensemble, *The King's Singers,* who, after infant baptism and confirmation in the Church of England and several years as a regular communicant, sought baptism in a Baptist Church 'as a witness that Jesus Christ was now Lord of my life, in a way that he had never been before'.[4]

The fact that baptist churches have often been willing to administer 'baptism' to a person already baptized has been a bone of contention between the denominations for centuries. That it is still an issue which arouses controversy is revealed by the letters which *Crusade* published in response to the article about Mr Perrin.[5] The position of the paedobaptist churches is clear, and can be stated in three sentences. Baptism is unrepeatable. Infant baptism is valid. No 'second baptism' is possible. Baptists would agree that baptism is unrepeatable, but some would argue that infant baptism is invalid and therefore the 'second baptism' is really the first and only valid baptism

Some ministers in paedobaptist denominations have been under pressure in recent years to administer believers' baptism to people baptized in infancy who, after conversion, feel that they ought to be baptized in this way. The Ministerial Session of the Methodist Conference has discussed this problem, which undoubtedly causes pastoral difficulties for ministers who receive such requests.

Although the requests cause difficulties, however, the paedobaptist is able to defend his practice on grounds such as those suggested in Chapter Three. If the person seeking believers' baptism objects that his own upbringing hardly justified the value placed by paedobaptists on the role of parents, it can be pointed out to him that, in the providence of God, he has now come to have faith for himself. God's prevenient grace has been available to him throughout his life; he has now responded to it. What he is lacking is not the sacrament of baptism, but an understanding of the way in which it relates to his present experience. He is more concerned with

[3] December 1976, pp.46–9
[4] Ibid., p.49
[5] February 1977, p.11; March 1977, p.4; April 1977, p.6

his own subjective feelings than with God's objective act. He must be helped to come to a more objective understanding of baptism. As John Stacey says:

> In the diversity of theology and practice in the universal Church believers' baptism and infant baptism both have their place. What is entirely unacceptable is that people who are baptized already should be 'baptized' again. This is to substitute personal experience for the grace of God, and virtually to tell the good Lord that his first attempt was not good enough.[6]

While the paedobaptist churches are undoubtedly correct in defending their position in this way, the subjective element in baptism should not be treated as unimportant. If we consider the case of a child whose parents have him baptized only for reasons of convention, who has no further contact with the Church until his late teens, and who at that age experiences conversion, we can perhaps sympathize with the question:

> Is it right to baptize an infant and, by doing so, possibly take away from him the privilege and thrill of being baptized at a later date, as a profession of his own personal faith in the Lord Jesus Christ? [7]

In the circumstances we have described, it is much more likely that a person will feel the need for a service which testifies to his newly found faith; it is much less likely that this need will be felt in the case of a child born into a practising Christian family. The latter, if the teaching offered by Church and parents is what it should be, will be helped to relate his growing religious experience to what happened in his baptism, and he will discover that baptism has 'so much of the gospel in it that it repays continual recall and affectionate meditation'.[8] He is most unlikely, therefore, to request a 'meaningful' baptism. But not all the baptized receive such careful nurture:

[6] John Stacey, op. cit., p.336

[7] Ian R. Sim in *Crusade,* March 1977, p.4

[8] J. Neville Ward in the symposium, *Doing Theology,* The Local Preachers' Department of the Methodist Church, 1972, p.187

Indiscriminate infant baptism penalizes the recipients of the rite
. . . The point of penalizing is if and when youngsters from unbe-
lieving homes ever become Christians. If so, it will be by genuine
conversion, not by Christian upbringing. And if this is so, then the
conversion should be marked, established and sealed by baptism.
A new convert is most likely to need this point of no return
provided in baptism, and has difficulty in understanding the value
of a far past infant baptism which never brought him into actual
relationship with God or his people.[9]

Buchanan is not arguing for 're-baptism' in such cases, but for
a strict baptismal policy which would prevent such cases
occurring. The case for and against such a policy will be
presented more fully in Part Two of the present work; all that
is necessary here is to observe that the relationship between
baptism and conversion varies from person to person and that
'indiscriminate' infant baptism can cause difficulties when
some of its recipients later experience conversion.

Confirmation

Does the theology of confirmation imply that, in some sense,
baptism is incomplete until it is confirmed?[10]

This is a very important question, and one which cannot be
avoided in any discussion of Christian initiation. As we have
seen,[11] the origins of confirmation are to be found in the early
Church, when baptism was immediately followed by anointing with oil and laying on of hands and prayer for the gift of
the Holy Spirit. In the West, for reasons of expediency, these
actions and prayers became separated from baptism, and in
the course of time, that which had been adopted for practical
purposes was justified theologically. What, then, is the relationship between baptism and confirmation?
Some scholars, notably Gregory Dix[12] and L. S.

---

[9] Colin O. Buchanan, *Baptismal Discipline,* Grove Booklets, Second Edition,
1974, p.16 (cited hereafter as Buchanan, *Discipline*)
[10] From a 1973 Report of a Special Committee of the Church of Scotland, quoted
in *Worship and the Child,* edited by R. C. D. Jasper, S.P.C.K., 1975, p.28
[11] See above p.38
[12] Dom Gregory Dix, *The Theology of Confirmation in Relation to Baptism,* Dacre
Press, 1946

Thornton,[13] have argued that confirmation, as practised in New Testament times, although normally associated with baptism, had a separate significance. Baptism was concerned with cleansing and with participation in Christ's death and resurrection; confirmation was concerned with reception of the Holy Spirit. On this view, baptism is indeed incomplete, and confirmation is extremely important. Thus Thornton writes:

> Unconfirmed Christians, it would seem, have not yet entered into the full mercies of the Covenant.[14]

If Thornton is right, a serious difficulty is presented to the Western churches, who, unlike the Orthodox churches, separate baptism from confirmation by a number of years, and thus deviate from the original practice of the Church. For, as Quick says,

> A theory which declares that confirmation marks the first gift of the indwelling Spirit, and a practice which places confirmation a dozen years or more after baptism, point, when taken together, to conclusions which are intolerable.[15]

Either the theology is wrong, and confirmation does not mark the first indwelling of the Spirit; or the practice is wrong, and confirmation should be administered as originally, immediately after baptism.

The majority of scholars, however, have rejected Dix's and Thornton's view. Flemington, for example, has strong reservations about the New Testament evidence:

> There is evidence ... in the Acts of the Apostles and in the Epistle to the Hebrews for the laying on of hands as a rite associated with, but distinguishable from, the rite of water-baptism. In Acts this laying on of hands is linked with the gift of the Holy Spirit, the clearest witness being afforded by Acts 8:14–17. But there is scarcely a mention of the rite elsewhere in the New Testament. St Paul's silence is particularly to be

[13] L. S. Thornton, *Confirmation Today,* Dacre Press, 1946
[14] Ibid., p.9
[15] Quick, op. cit., p.184

remarked . . . It is one thing to fail to refer to the laying on of hands, if it were an additional rite, practised in some quarters of the early Church. It is quite another thing to be utterly silent about it, if it were the rite with which the endowment of the Holy Spirit was pre-eminently and regularly associated. Had the laying on of hands formed the chief element in Christian initiation, it is hard to believe that St Paul could have failed to mention it.[16]

Paul's apparent failure to mention what Dix and Thornton claim to be a vital part of initiation is rendered even more remarkable by the fact that he so frequently refers to baptism.[17] Thornton, however, believes that the New Testament references to 'sealing' with the Holy Spirit relate to the post-baptismal rite rather than to baptism itself.[18] Against this view, Lampe has asserted that these passages refer to the initiation-act in its entirety and denies that confirmation was in any sense separate from baptism in apostolic times or had a separate meaning.[19]

The weight of scholarly opinion now favours the view that, although the origins of confirmation are to be found in the ceremonies which, in New Testament practice, immediately followed baptism, no separate theology of confirmation is to be found in the New Testament, and in particular, the gift of the Spirit is associated with the total act of initiation, of which baptism constituted the major part. The wide acceptance with which Lampe's argument has been greeted has led to a number of attempts to re-assess the significance of confirmation.

In 1971, the document popularly known as the *Ely Report*[20]

concluded that baptism is the one rite of initiation into the Christian Church. It went on to recommend radical alterations in the service of confirmation which would remove the idea that it marked the reception of the Holy Spirit in the baptized.[21]

[16] Flemington, op. cit., p.149
[17] See above, pp.16-21, 26f.
[18] Thornton, op. cit., pp.7f.
[19] See above, p.23
[20] *Christian Initiation, Birth and Growth in the Christian Society,* Church Information Office, 1971
[21] Bridge and Phypers, op. cit., p.160

Such alterations are, however, only one of the possibilities. Another, which would find favour in some quarters, would be the abandonment of confirmation altogether:

> The radical approach of the Ely Report to the problems presented by confirmation enjoys the support of some evangelical Anglican writers. They have contended that if paedobaptism is true baptism it must indeed have the same meaning for infants as for adults. Confirmation is thus an unscriptural and irrelevant appendage and must go, to be replaced by an annual service of ratification of baptismal vows attended by all baptized adults.[22]

Or confirmation could be applied to infants at the time of their baptism, as occurs in the East. After all, as O. C. Quick pointed out as long ago as 1927, 'the theological arguments against confirming infants seem to be equally strong against baptizing them'.[23] If the case for infant baptism can be upheld, should not infant confirmation also be considered?

To deal with the last suggestion first: if Lampe is right in associating the gift of the Holy Spirit with baptism rather than confirmation and the *Ely Report* is correct in asserting that 'baptism is the one rite of initiation into the Christian Church', nothing would be gained by adding infant confirmation to infant baptism. On the other hand (and this is also an objection to the suggestion that confirmation should be entirely abolished), confirmation a number of years after baptism *can* have positive value, provided that the inflated view of its importance, suggested by Dix and Thornton, is disregarded.

What then is the value of confirmation? The original meaning of the English word 'confirm' is 'strengthen'; and strengthening is an activity that is particularly associated with the Holy Spirit, the Paraclete. Although the Spirit is present at baptism and active throughout a person's development, it is not inappropriate to invoke his help in private devotion and corporate worship; and it seems specially

[22] Ibid., pp. 160f.
[23] Quick, op. cit., p. 183

desirable that in adolescence, when confirmation usually takes place, such invocation for the confirming (strengthening) work of the Spirit should be made both by the candidate and by the Church. What Quick says of his own Anglican Church is probably true also of other denominations which practise confirmation:

> It is most unlikely that the Church of England will consent to forego an established custom which may be, and often is, of such incalculable value as a means of giving strength to the young life about to face, or perhaps already facing, the trials of adolescence, or of 'going out to work'.[24]

In general, the Western Church has looked upon confirmation as a strengthening ordinance which 'confers further graces of the Spirit, especially for growth and stability in the Christian life . . . but nothing other in kind or in essential principle from what baptism has already given'.[25] As the Second Vatican Council puts it, Christians are

> incorporated into Christ's Mystical Body through baptism and strengthened by the power of the Holy Spirit through confirmation.[26]

'The major work in confirmation is that of the Holy Spirit.'[27] But the word 'confirmation' has a secondary meaning, that of ratification or endorsement, which also has some bearing on the theology of confirmation. There is a sense in which the person being confirmed is also confirming something. He is declaring that he is happy to belong to the Church into whose family he was received many years previously. Thus

> the individual concerned has the opportunity, by his personal commitment and profession of faith in Christ, of sharing in the confirmation of that which was done for him at his baptism.[28]

[24] Ibid.
[25] Ibid., p.182
[26] *The Documents of Vatican II*, edited by Walter M. Abbott, S.J., Geoffrey Chapman, 1967, p.492
[27] John Stacey, op. cit., p.337
[28] Ibid.

This opportunity to 'confirm one's baptism' is extremely valuable, particularly when it follows a conversion experience or a realization by a baptized person that he genuinely cherishes his place in Christ's Church. Confirmation is both backward-looking and forward-looking; the candidate thankfully recalls his baptism and the providence of God which has brought him to his present experience and, at the same time, re-dedicates himself for future discipleship.

Our proposed theology of confirmation is relatively modest. We do not claim that confirmation is an essential part of Christian initiation, still less that it is the major part, without which baptism is incomplete. But we maintain that it has considerable value as a rite in which a person baptized in infancy can testify to the faith which is necessary to make his relationship with God a living reality, can confirm his place within the Body of Christ, and can pledge his future loyalty, while he prays, together with his fellow-members of the Body, that he may be strengthened by the Holy Spirit to continue in God's service.

How is confirmation understood within Methodism? It is only recently that Methodism adopted the word 'confirmation', having previously used certain phrases about 'membership'. Two terms, 'confirmation' and 'reception into full membership' are now used interchangeably. The latter reflects Methodism's origins as a Society rather than a church. In the eighteenth century, 'membership of the Church and membership of a Methodist Society were two different things'.[29] The first Methodists counted themselves members of the Church by baptism but they were made members of a Society if they showed evidence of a desire 'to flee from the wrath to come'. And, in the words of Donald English:

> Methodism has continued to have the characteristics of a Society even after she became established as a church ... The societary element has focused attention upon the concept of membership as being entered into by those who, having considered the implications, having been properly trained, and having the necessary

[29] Donald English in *Epworth Review*, May 1974, p.70

(experiential) qualification and evidences, consciously and publicly commit themselves to belonging to the Church in general and the local Society in particular. The sacramental element is prior, since all who are received into membership are already baptized. But it is neither dominant nor central.[30]

This assessment of the relative importance of baptism and reception into full membership may be true of Methodism *inasmuch as it remains a Society,* but, as English points out, Methodism is also a church. This double identity, claims a 1963 report,[31] provides the denomination with a great advantage but is also the cause of 'certain inconveniences and confusions'. One such confusion surrounds the word 'membership'. In what sense is membership conferred by baptism? In what sense is it conferred in the reception service? (Or, indeed, to what extent does the vote of the Church Council make a person a member?) The 1936 reception service is entitled *The Order of Service for the Public Reception of New Members,* which appears to imply that baptism does *not* make a person a member of the Church. But this is not necessarily the case. In fact, the 1936 service is far from clear about the matter:

> At your baptism you were received into the congregation of Christ's flock . . . We are here present . . . to welcome you into the fellowship of his Holy Church.

What, we may well ask, is the difference between 'the congregation of Christ's flock' and 'the fellowship of his Holy Church'? A difference *seems* to be implied, for these are *new* members. The explanation seems to lie in the concept of the Society. Although it is said that the 'new' members are being received into the Church, the notion of new membership of the Society lies behind the service. If this is not so, the language is inexplicable: if a person has been received, by baptism, 'into the congregation of Christ's flock', he must *in some sense* be a member of the Church. How then can he be described as a 'new' member?

[30] Ibid., pp.70f.
[31] The Methodist Conference Church Membership Report, 1963, quoted by English, op. cit., p.70

Donald English, however, makes a different comment on the apparent distinction between 'flock' and 'Church':

> Since the 1952 statement makes clear that baptism admits to the One, Holy, Catholic and Apostolic Church, into the household of faith, the distinguishing feature of the membership service appears to be in the words, 'In taking your place'. The distinction implied is not reception into two different areas, but between *being accepted without choice* and *choosing to be accepted.* In view of their response to the call of Christ to follow him they now take their place and are welcomed into the fellowship.[32]

If this is so, there is little difference in meaning, though much in terminology, between the 1936 service and the account which we have given above of the relationship between confirmation and baptism. The candidate for reception is now choosing to be accepted, having previously been accepted without choice. But the question whether a child can be said to be a member of the Church by virtue of his baptism, *and to what extent,* still cannot be disregarded.

More recent services, in 1967 and 1974, while abandoning the imprecise term 'new members' have adopted in its place the term 'full members'. The implication of this term is not that baptism does not confer membership, but that the membership conferred by baptism is incomplete. Here again, the societary element in Methodism's heritage has made its mark. Even if a person is a member of the Church by baptism, he is not eligible to vote in elections at the General Church Meeting or to serve on certain committees until he is received into the full membership of the Church. But there is a deeper sense in which the use of the term can be defended:

> Since an infant is incapable of entering into conscious fellowship with the Lord and his people, the (baptized) child's membership is necessarily incomplete.[33]

> The question is sometimes put . . . whether baptism is complete in itself. It is complete in that it is the only sacrament divinely

[32] Ibid., p.73
[33] Memorandum on Infant Baptism, Methodist Conference *Minutes,* 1936, pp.400f.

instituted for this purpose, and is in itself an effective sign of all the blessings of the new covenant; it is also, however, incomplete, as our Methodist emphasis on conversion reminds us, in that these blessings need to be appropriated by faith; it is proleptic; it sums up that which has to be progressively realized.[34]

This is a valid point. But the difficulties raised by the term 'full membership' are still not entirely overcome. For Bernard Jones has recently presented a case for regarding membership of the Church as a *process* rather than as a single event, associated with either baptism or confirmation, or as a combination of the two:

> The important point is that membership is a constantly growing and changing relationship. Perhaps the Church has failed to show clearly that membership is not a status but a relationship, a growing relationship with Christ and his people. A confirmation certificate must not be thought of as a kind of 'A' level certificate in the Christian faith. It is more like a passport for further travel. Confirmation must be seen as the initiation of a further stage of growth rather than as simply the completion of baptism.[35]

This is a helpful way of looking at the subject under discussion and one which fully accords with what we have previously said about the importance of post-baptismal faith and the necessity for the baptized to become what he is. The Christian life is an ongoing process of development, punctuated indeed by specific events such as baptism and confirmation, but never, on this side of eternity, coming to a full stop. Infant baptism (and, for that matter, believers' baptism) can be said to be incomplete inasmuch as there is enormous potential for further growth in discipleship. At baptism the pilgrimage has barely begun. Yet even this does not resolve the difficulties which are presented by the term 'full membership', for if those who take the view that baptism admits to the full membership of the Church assert that the expression over-emphasizes confirmation at the expense of baptism, supporters of the 'process' approach of Jones can assert that it

[34] Report on Church Membership, Methodist Conference *Agenda,* 1961, p.38
[35] Bernard Jones, *Belonging,* Epworth Press, 1973, p.38. For Jones's general discussion of initiation, see pp.26–51

claims too much for confirmation at the expense of ongoing Christian development.

Perhaps this discussion must lead us to the conclusion that the difficulty is one of terminology rather than of theology in the strict sense. It appears that Methodism, in adopting 'full' in place of 'new', has jumped out of the frying-pan into the fire. As we have seen, the concept of membership is precious to Methodism for historical reasons, but it is obvious that the continued use of the word unnecessarily clouds the theological issues. The recent use of the word 'confirmation' is to be preferred on these grounds, quite apart from the fact that it is used by certain other denominations. If we wish to understand what Methodism means by 'Confirmation, or Reception into Full Membership', we shall be enabled to do so more effectively if we examine the relevant service rather than quibble about its title. This will be part of our concern in Chapter Five.

Communion
The usual practice of the Church of England is to baptize people in infancy, confirm them as adolescents, and then admit them to communion. Those who 'slip through the net' in adolescence and are not confirmed, although they may thereafter become regular worshippers, do not communicate. Communion is for the confirmed. Methodism has no clear rules about the matter, but has applied the same system, by and large, to children. Unconfirmed adults, however, who have wished to communicate, have not generally been discouraged from doing so, though ministers have often taken the opportunity to encourage them to become full members. The United Reformed Church and the Church of Scotland also tend to think of participation in the eucharist as the privilege of full members, or at least of adults. But there now appears to be a growing body of opinion within all these churches that baptism rather than confirmation properly admits a person to communicant status.

What we have said about baptism and confirmation constitutes a *prima facie* case for the view that all the baptized are eligible to communicate, regardless of their age. If baptism admits to the membership of the Church, does it not also admit to full participation in the Church's principal act of worship? If baptism is a sacrament to which the ordinance of confirmation is subordinate, should it not be the sacrament, rather than the ordinance, that entitles a person to share in the other dominical sacrament?

Apart from the theology of initiation, certain practical factors have lent force to the argument that baptized children should be allowed to communicate. One of the fruits of the Liturgical Movement has been an increased emphasis on the centrality of the eucharist. Parish churches which used to have Mattins as the principal Sunday morning service, preceded by an earlier celebration of the eucharist for the specially devout, now tend to make the Parish eucharist the principal act of worship. Methodism and the Free Churches in general have also re-discovered the importance of the eucharist and have started to celebrate it more frequently than before—weekly, in some churches. As a result of this renewed awareness of the eucharist, the practice of involving children to a considerable though limited extent in communion services has grown. In many churches, children are encouraged to be present, usually after the Ministry of the Word, to witness the eucharistic actions, to share in the prayers, and to come to the communion rail with their parents or Sunday school teachers. At the rail, however, they receive, not the eucharistic elements, but a blessing.

These factors have made the discussion about child communion not merely an interesting academic exercise but a practical, pastoral issue. What possible reason can there be for withholding the elements from someone who belongs to the Church by baptism? Why should adults receive the bread and wine, while children receive a blessing? Furthermore, there is evidence that some children keenly feel the deprivation. Their parents and teachers receive the elements; so, maybe, do their older brothers and sisters; why should they be denied? Other ministers may have shared the experience of the present writer, who, about to give a blessing to a child, has seen him stretch out his hands in the (forlorn) hope of receiving the bread. To refuse him seems tantamount to an assertion that the child does not fully belong to the worshipping community. As Jones says, it is vital that the youngster should feel that he belongs at every point. In the development of young people the age of eleven or twelve seems to be crucial. This is why many people argue for confirmation at this age. Others point out that at this age the child is not ready for the commitment that full membership implies but that he might be ready, with suitable preparation, for his first communion. Confirmation and the assumption of voting rights would follow later.[36]

There must be many children, who have accompanied their parents to the communion rail, who reach a stage described by Dr John Robinson. 'They were not nearly ready for confirmation but they were ready for communion.'[37]

The admission of children to communion is not unknown in the Church. The Eastern churches administer communion to infants (though these infants have already received chrism); the Roman Catholic Church considers that at about the age of seven years children are ready to make their first communion.[38] John Wesley sometimes administered communion to children, 'though only after the most careful enquiry'.[39] Many churches are currently considering the matter.

In the Church of England,

the outcome of this debate could be the earlier admission of children to Holy Communion . . . This earlier reception would be preceded by instruction, but such preparation would not be couched in the 'life-vows' terms that much confirmation teaching has contained in the past.[40]

The Church of Scotland has been moved to ask:

Is confirmation necessary before admission to the Lord's Supper? Must admission depend on a single, formal confession of faith and commitment for life, or can it depend on an appropriate confession of faith before each communion? . . . If the latter, can any age limit be fixed, below which it would be reasonable to assume that a child would be incapable of real personal faith

---

[36] Ibid., p.40
[37] Ibid., p.32
[38] See *Worship and the Child*, p.34
[39] Methodist Conference *Agenda*, 1975, p.256
[40]*Worship and the Child*, p.21

in Jesus Christ? If a child is capable of real faith, is it right to exclude him from the benefits of communion as a means of grace, and if so, what are the actual grounds of such exclusion? . . . There is at least a *prima facie* case for a careful look at the possibility of admitting children to communion.[41]

The Methodist Youth Department presented a report to the Methodist Conference in 1973 which discussed some of the advantages and disadvantages of administering communion to children. Although it recommended flexibility of practice rather than a general policy of admitting children to communion, it noted that

for some young people their first communion may mark an important stage in their developing commitment towards full membership.[42]

This report was followed in 1975 by a report from the Faith and Order Committee which set out detailed arguments for and against the admission of children to communion, but reached no definite conclusion:

The Committee asks Conference to accept this statement as an account of the issues involved and to commend it for study. The Committee does not wish to stress either the values or the disadvantages of flexibility and experiment to the exclusion of the other; and recognizing that the present custom of Methodism is to avoid excessive rigidity in such matters it recommends the Conference to take no constitutional action in the matter.[43]

Clearly the issue of child communion is engaging the attention of the paedobaptist churches. Not only the *prima facie* case for such a practice has been noted, however, but also some of the difficulties. The Roman Catholic Church administers communion to children when they reach 'the age of discretion' at about seven years, not from infancy. Most of the arguments for administering communion to children assume that there will be 'real personal faith in Jesus Christ' on the part of the communicants:

[41] Ibid., p.28
[42] Methodist Conference *Agenda*, 1973, pp.11f.
[43] Methodist Conference *Agenda*, 1975, p.261

If it is being argued that children could not *understand* what they are doing in receiving the eucharistic gifts, then we as adults are making the most arrogant claims about our own understanding of what can only be described as one of the most profound of all mysteries. Surely we have begun to learn that it is folly to try and simplify the eucharist into the inadequacies of human description. Even so it seems to be that the thought-forms of the child are more often able to pierce the fog of theological debate which too often surrounds our talk about the Holy Communion. For them there is no difficulty in 'discerning the Lord'. The sacramental principle is not one which is as foreign to the child's mind as it is to many sophisticated adults.[44]

These words of Donald Gray may well be true of children, even very young children, but they can hardly be applied to infants. Yet the logic of the theological argument (though not the pastoral arguments) in favour of child communion also demands infant communion. The baptized infant belongs to the Body, to the Christian Family, just as much as his four-year-old brother, who is able to 'pierce the fog'. Some writers, notably Colin Buchanan, are happy to follow the argument to its logical conclusion.[45] But there is little evidence to suggest that the major churches are in any way ready for such a momentous change of practice.

Further difficulties might well arise in practice. A Sunday school may include one or two children who have not been baptized. If baptism is the criterion for communicant membership of the Church, such children could not communicate; yet to draw a distinction between baptized and unbaptized children would have the most unfortunate consequences. Other very young children, baptized in infancy, might belong to homes in which no Christian nurture was provided apart from the act of sending the children to Sunday school; yet 'admission to communion for an infant or very young child can only be done by extending the parents' status of communicants to the child'.[46] A strict baptismal policy, such as will be discussed in Part Two, might well resolve the second difficulty in due time, but it could also have the effect of adding to the

[44] *Worship and the Child*, p.18
[45] Buchanan, *A Case*, p.19
[46] Buchanan, *Discipline*, p.9

first, by increasing the number of unbaptized children attending Sunday school (unless, of course, it had the effect of deterring parents not only from having their children baptized but also from sending them to Sunday school). Another possibility would be for communicant parents to be invited to bring their children to evening communion services at which all could communicate, but this would entail the disadvantage that other children associated with the Church through Sunday school could not witness celebrations of the eucharist as they often do at present unless the two practices were to be retained side by side (which would be ludicrous) and it would also make a distinction among the baptized. The only *practicable* solution would be to allow only children who were thought capable of faith and understanding to communicate, taking care to baptize them at this stage if they had not previously been baptized, and to disallow infant communion. But whether this is *theologically* defensible is, as we have seen, doubtful.

These problems will require considerable attention, such as the initiation debate as a whole is receiving, before any clear solutions are found. There is a good theological case for admitting children of all ages to communion on the strength of baptism, but the difficulties of reconciling practice and theology are considerable. Some of these difficulties might be overcome by experience if what is a very new practice in the West is extended; flexibility and controlled experiment should therefore be welcomed.

CHAPTER FIVE

Entry into the Church in Methodist Liturgy

PREVIOUS chapters of the present work have argued that infant baptism is consistent with New Testament theology and have sought to relate the theology of baptism to Christian experience, to confirmation, and to participation in the eucharist. Most church members, however, do not encounter the theology of initiation by reading books and articles on the subject, but by being present at services of baptism and confirmation. It is obviously important, therefore, that we should examine the current Methodist services of baptism and confirmation to see to what extent they reflect the account of initiation which we have presented.

During the late 1960s the Methodist Church authorized the use of a number of 'experimental' forms of service for the sacraments and certain other ordinances, in order that their suitability might be assessed by the Church. Services of this sort for baptism (both of infants and of those able to answer for themselves) and confirmation appeared in 1967. After a period of experimentation and consultation, revised forms of service were authorized by the Methodist Conference in 1974 and published in *The Methodist Service Book*[1] in the following year. In this chapter, our main concern will be to examine the 1974 services of initiation (grouped together in the service book under the general heading 'Entry into the Church'), though occasional references to their predecessors of 1967 and 1936 and to the recent rites of some other denominations will also be necessary.

---

[1] For a commentary on *The Methodist Service Book* (referred to hereafter as *M.S.B.*), see Neil Dixon, *At Your Service*, Epworth Press, 1976

The Baptism of Infants

The structure of this service is worthy of note. In common with other new Methodist services it proceeds, after an act of Preparation, through the Ministry of the Word, to an act of Response. This structure, always appropriate for worship, is particularly so in the case of baptism. It emphasizes the priority of grace: only when God has spoken can man respond; it is only when Jesus says 'Follow me' that discipleship becomes possible. 'The New Testament tells of men hearing the Word of God expounded, responding to it, and being baptized'.[2] The reading and proclamation of the scriptures is the liturgical expression of the gracious initiative of God; response then follows in prayer, promises, profession of faith, and the act of baptism.

A special baptismal collect is provided in the Preparation:

Heavenly Father, we thank you that in every generation you give new sons and daughters to your Church, and we pray that this child, now to be received by baptism, may know you better and love you more day by day, through Jesus Christ our Lord.[3]

The phrase 'new sons and daughters' immediately suggests rebirth, although baptismal regeneration is not explicitly mentioned. Nevertheless, the idea that children are born into, incorporated into, the family of the Church by baptism is strongly suggested. But the main thrust of the prayer is forward-looking, with a petition for an ever-increasing awareness of and responsiveness to God on the part of the child. God's prevenient grace is hinted at in the first sentence. God gives children to his Church. We belong to the Church not primarily because we wish to do so, but because God has given us to the Church. Thus, in this collect, several important New Testament insights into the meaning of baptism are expressed.

Three short passages from the Gospels are appointed to be read, each of them significant. The first is Mark's account of the baptism of Jesus, rightly included if 'the baptism of Jesus . . . is of central importance for an understanding of the

---

[2] Ibid., p.48
[3] *M.S.B.,* p.A6

Church's baptism'.[4] This reading was absent from the 1936
service (which in this respect follows *The Book of Common
Prayer*) and the 1967 rite; and it is interesting to observe in
passing that it is also absent from the Anglican *Series 3*,
though it had been included in *Series 2* and is found in the
Roman Catholic rite. The second Gospel, which was also
included in the earlier Methodist services, is the controversial
pericope in Mark 10 about Jesus receiving and blessing the
children. *Series 3* omits this reading because of 'the difficulties
felt by some scholars in accepting that this story has anything
to do with baptism' and because it has been felt that the
passage can more appropriately be used in the *Series 3* service
of *Thanksgiving for the Birth of a Child*.[5] The third Gospel
reading, common to all the Methodist services and to the
recent Roman and Anglican rites, is Matthew's account of the
apostles' commission to preach and baptize.

These three Gospels, taken together, proclaim that Christian baptism owes its existence to the baptism of Jesus and his
commission to the Church, and that children have a place
within God's kingdom. The readings are followed by a brief
exposition of their significance for the Church's practice:

> Thus the children of Christian parents are brought to be baptized
> with water as a sign of the new life in Christ, and to be made
> members of God's family the Church. We bring this child whom
> God has entrusted to us and claim for him all that Christ has won
> for us. Christ loves him and is ready to receive him, to embrace
> him with the arms of his mercy and to give him the blessing of
> eternal life.[6]

This exposition contains several important phrases which
deserve particular attention. It is the children of *'Christian
parents'* who are presented for baptism. Part Two of this book
is largely devoted to a discussion of the issues raised by this
term and there is no need for us to enlarge upon the matter
here, except to remark that the presence of the word 'Christ-

---

[4] Arndt, op. cit., p.38
[5] *Alternative Services Series 3, Initiation Services*, A Report by the Liturgical
Commission of the Church of England, S.P.C.K., 1977, p.10. (This document is cited
hereafter as *Series 3*.)
[6] *M.S.B.*, p.A7

ian' is clearly significant. It would have been easy enough to say 'Thus children are brought to be baptized . . .' if the Methodist Church had so wished. *'To be made members of God's family the Church'* is another revealing phrase. The ambiguity which we observed in the 1935 reception service[7] has now disappeared, and membership of the Church is clearly stated to be a consequence of baptism. (There is, however, a lingering reference to 'full membership' later in the baptismal service.) Baptism is *'a sign of the new life in Christ'*. This statement is less strongly worded than its counterparts in other contemporary liturgies; *Series 3*, for example, declares that baptism is the 'sign and seal of this new birth'.[8] But it is very difficult, as well as being foreign to biblical thought,[9] to make a sharp distinction between symbol and instrument, a fact to which the historic controversies surrounding both dominical sacraments amply testify. The suggestion that this phrase implies that baptism is 'mere symbolism' is perhaps dispelled by the statement that we *'claim for him all that Christ has won for us'*. Baptism is here linked with the great events which secured mankind's salvation, supremely the death and resurrection of Christ, and baptism claims salvation for the baptized. The final sentence refers back to the Gospel about Jesus blessing the children, and thus stresses the appropriateness of presenting an infant for baptism.

There is, however, a significant omission from the 1974 exposition. The 1967 version, closely followed in 1974, included the words 'The children of Christian parents are brought to be baptized with water as a sign of cleansing'.[10] 'A sign of cleansing' has been replaced in the 1974 service by 'a sign of the new life in Christ'. As we have noted,[11] not all paedobaptists are happy to apply the concept of baptismal cleansing to infant baptism, though *Series 3* is not afraid to include in its baptismal prayer 'Bless this water, that your servants who are washed in it may be made one with Christ'.[12]

[7] See above, pp.78–82
[8] *Series 3*, p.31
[9] See above, pp.15, 27f.
[10] *Entry into the Church*, Methodist Publishing House, 1967, p.7
[11] See above, pp.59f.
[12] *Series 3*, p.33

The striking omission of the phrase in 1974 seems to reflect the fact that some Methodists hesitate to speak about baptism as a means of cleansing from original sin; it should, therefore, be taken as an indication of Methodism's view that it is not essential to regard infant baptism as an act of cleansing.

The baptismal prayer, after thanksgiving for the mighty acts of God in creation and redemption, includes a number of significant petitions:

> Father, be present with us in the power of your Spirit. We pray that this child, now to be baptized in this water, may die to sin and be raised to the new life in Christ.[13]

Here the Pauline conception of baptism as participation in Christ's death and resurrection finds its first expression in the service. The hope that the baptized child may come to have personal faith is then embodied in the words:

> We pray that he may learn to trust Jesus Christ as his Lord and Saviour.[14]

The work of the Holy Spirit, who is active in baptism itself ('be present with us in the power of your Spirit'), will need to continue in the baptized throughout his development, especially if he is to share in Christ's conquest of evil:

> We pray that by the power of the Holy Spirit he may have victory over evil.[15]

Finally, the prayer expresses the biblical thought that baptism marks a transition, or the beginning of a transition, from one life to another:

> From darkness lead him to light, from death lead him to eternal life . . .[16]

[13] *M.S.B.*, p.A8
[14] Ibid.
[15] Ibid.
[16] Ibid.

These petitions make clear the important theological truth that, although (or perhaps because) baptism is a once-for-all event, it is able to sum up the whole Christian pilgrimage. Death and resurrection, victory over evil, faith, the work of the Holy Spirit in the baptized—of all these baptism is the symbol and the instrument. The Christian life is a process of growing into that which baptism declares the baptized to be, participants in the new life in Christ.

Before the parents are asked to give their promises, there is an opportunity for the local congregation to reply to the question:

> Members of the household of faith, who are now in his name to receive this child, will you so maintain the common life of worship and service that he and all the children among you may grow in grace and in the knowledge and love of God and of his Son Jesus Christ our Lord?[17]

This question, which has no equivalent in Roman Catholic or Anglican rites, is very valuable. It serves to underline the fact that baptism is a sacrament of the Church, incorporation into a Body whose limbs and organs depend upon one another. The Church, through its local representatives, has great responsibility for those who are baptized, and, for their spiritual growth, the baptized are to a large extent dependent upon the nurture provided by such local fellowships of Christians. It is also worth noting that because baptism is a sacrament of the Church it should be administered at a time when the local congregation is gathered for worship, rather than in isolation from the worshipping community. The provision of a promise for the congregation to make emphasizes the importance of the congregation's presence and thus reinforces the General Direction which indicates that baptism should normally be administered at a service of public worship.[18]

The promises of the parents, which follow that of the congregation, are concerned with the nurture that will be provided for the child:

[17] Ibid., pp.A8f.
[18] Ibid., p.A3

You have brought this child to be baptized, and you will receive him again to be trained in the doctrines, privileges and duties of the Christian religion. I ask you therefore:

Will you provide for this your child a Christian home of love and faithfulness? (Answer: With God's help we will.)

Will you help him by your words, prayers and example to renounce all evil and to put his trust in Jesus Christ his Saviour? (Answer: With God's help we will.)

Will you encourage him to enter into the full membership of the Church, and to serve Christ in the world? (Answer: With God's help we will.)[19]

These questions have their counterparts in Roman Catholic and Anglican services; but in those rites parents and god-parents are also asked to declare on their own behalf and on behalf of the child that they turn to Christ and renounce evil, and to profess faith in each of the Persons of the Trinity. This may be illustrated from *Series 3*:

Do you turn to Christ? (Answer: I turn to Christ.)
Do you repent of your sins? (Answer: I repent of my sins.)
Do you renounce evil? (Answer: I renounce evil.) . . .

Do you believe and trust in God the Father, the maker of all? (Answer: I believe and trust in him.)
Do you believe and trust in his Son, Jesus Christ, the redeemer of the world? (Answer: I believe and trust in him.)
Do you believe and trust in his Holy Spirit, the giver of life? (Answer: I believe and trust in him.)[20]

These questions in *Series 3* demand an explicit profession of Christian faith by the parents, to which there is no exact parallel in the Methodist rite. If it is agreed that baptism should be administered to infants partly on the grounds that their parents have faith, there is good reason to think that the Anglican and Roman Catholic approach is preferable to that of Methodism and that the absence of a direct and personal profession of faith on the part of parents from the rite which

[19] Ibid., p.A9
[20] *Series 3*, pp.32f.

we are studying is to be regretted. On the other hand, the Methodist promises, properly understood, surely pre-suppose faith. Is 'a Christian home of love and faithfulness' capable of existing in the absence of faith? How can parents hope to fulfil the second promise if they themselves do not speak of Jesus, say their prayers, renounce evil and trust in Christ? What sort of encouragement can they give a child to enter 'into the full membership of the Church, and to serve Christ in the world' if they are not themselves similarly com-mitted? If the Methodist service does not require parents explicitly to profess faith, it asks them to make promises which assume that they have it.

There is reason to regret the absence of a specific profes-sion of faith by the parents, but there is a positive advantage in the promises, in that, by emphasizing the importance of nur-ture, they underline the fact that Christian discipleship is an ongoing and developing relationship, in which the influence and example of parents is very significant.

Methodism made no provisions for godparents in 1936; and they are not essential in the 1974 service, though spon-sors may be appointed if it is desired. If there are sponsors, they do not join in the promises of the parents, as in Anglican and Roman Catholic rites, but give a separate promise to the effect that they will assist the parents in the child's Christian upbringing.

An opportunity for the whole congregation to confess the faith of the Church is presented by the provision in the service of the Apostles' Creed and a short summary which may be used as an alternative to the Creed. This is the faith into which the child is to be baptized; it is appropriate that it should be confessed.

After baptism itself and the making of the sign of the Cross, there is an optional ceremony of giving a lighted candle, the minister saying to the baptized child:

> I give you this sign, for you now belong to Christ, the light of the world.[21]

The child belongs to Christ because he is a member of the

[21] *M.S.B.,* p.A12

Body of Christ. He is a Member of the Body of Christ because he has been baptized. He has been baptized, in the presence of faith, in response to God's prevenient grace. God has given another son to the Church.

The final prayers reflect some of the themes which have previously been noted, thanking God for receiving the child within the family of the Church, praying that the child may grow up in and profess the faith in which he has been baptized, and asking that to this end his parents and the Church may be blessed and strengthened.

All the great New Testament emphases about baptism are to be found in the 1974 service with the single exception of cleansing. That omission, though regrettable, does not prevent the rite from being an admirable liturgical expression of the theology of baptism, entirely suitable for those to whom it purports to apply—'the children of Christian parents'.

Public Reception into Full Membership, or Confirmation
The confirmation service, like that of infant baptism, is structured in a way that makes it clear that God's grace precedes human response:

> Once again we see how good liturgy follows the logic of theology. Despite some appearances to the contrary, the Church is not a club which a man may join if he feels like it, and from which he may sever his connection at will. 'Jesus said to them, "Follow me".' His call comes to us; then we respond, for him or against him. This is the heart of confirmation theology: Jesus calls us to accept a place in his family, a place that has been reserved for us since we were baptized; we respond to that call; the Church publicly recognizes our response and admits us to the full membership of the family; by his Holy Spirit God strengthens us (confirms us) for his service.[22]

The confirmation collect in the 1974 service recognizes the operation of the Holy Spirit in the lives of the candidates and prays for its continuance:

> Heavenly Father, we thank you that by the preaching of the Gospel you have led these your servants to the knowledge of your

[22] Dixon, op. cit., p.54

truth; and we pray that the good work you have begun in them may be confirmed by the continued working of your Holy Spirit, through Jesus Christ our Lord.[23]

The Old Testament lesson (Jeremiah 31:31–34) proclaims that, in order to live in relationship to God, a man needs not only to be born into the covenant people but also to have inward knowledge of God. The candidates belong to the covenant by baptism, but baptism looks forward to the exercise of personal faith. The Epistle (Romans 8:12–17) discusses the work of the Holy Spirit in helping the sons of God to die and rise with Christ, to suffer with him in order to be glorified with him, and in testifying to them that they are indeed God's children. Mark 1:14–20, the appointed Gospel, describes how the fishermen of Galilee were called to be disciples and responded to that call. All three readings have an obvious appropriateness in the confirmation service.

Before the candidates profess their faith and make their promises, the minister addresses them in words which relate confirmation both to baptism and to Christian experience:

Beloved in Christ, at your baptism you were received into God's family the Church. You have grown in the knowledge and love of our Lord. You have heard Christ saying to you, as he said to his first disciples, Follow me. You have already responded to his call, and you come now by your own choice publicly to renounce evil and profess your faith in him. You are now to be confirmed as members of a chosen race, a royal priesthood, a holy nation, God's own people, sent forth as Christ's servants and witnesses into the world. For all this God will strengthen you by his Holy Spirit.[24]

This address, reproduced from the 1967 service without alteration, makes much clearer the relationship between baptism, confirmation and experience than does the 1935 service.[25] Baptism marks the beginning of the Christian life, reception into God's family. Growth in faith, knowledge and love follow; a most important feature of this growth is the realization that the call to discipleship is personal. Response

[23] *M.S.B.*, p.A17
[24] Ibid., p.A21
[25] See above, pp.78ff.

97

to the call leads to a personal decision to be confirmed as a member of the Church. Confirmation does not *make* a person a member of the 'chosen race . . .'; it *confirms* him as a member. And the Holy Spirit strengthens Jesus's disciples in order that they might serve him and bear witness to him. All this is entirely compatible with what we have said in Chapter Four[26] about the subordination of confirmation to baptism, the developing nature of Christian discipleship, the value of confirmation as a means whereby the candidate may confirm his place within the Church, and the continuing, confirming activity of the Holy Spirit.

The close relationship between baptism and confirmation is further demonstrated by the promises and the profession of faith. The three questions asked of the candidates reflect two of the promises given by parents in baptism:

Baptism[27]	*Confirmation*[28]
2. Will you help him . . . to renounce all evil and to put his trust in Jesus Christ his Saviour?	1. Do you repent of your sins and renounce all evil?
3. Will you encourage him to enter into the full membership of the Church, and to serve Christ in the world?	2. Do you trust in Jesus Christ as your Lord and Saviour?
	3. Will you obey Christ and serve him in the Church and in the world?

The Apostles' Creed, which may also be used in infant baptism, follows the questions and answers. This is the faith into which a child is baptized; in confirmation, it is the faith which he now personally professes, together with his fellow-members of Christ's Body.

The confirmation and reception proper begins with the confirmation prayer:

Heavenly Father, all-powerful God, who in baptism received these your children into your family, establish them now in faith by the Holy Spirit, and day by day increase in them your gifts of grace;

[26] See above, pp.73–82
[27] *M.S.B.*,p.A9
[28] Ibid., p.A22

the spirit of wisdom and understanding; Amen.
the spirit of counsel and might; Amen.
the spirit of knowledge and true godliness and the fear of the
Lord; Amen.
and keep them in your mercy for ever . . .
Lord, confirm your servant *N.* by your Holy Spirit that he may
continue to be yours for ever.[29]

Thus at the heart of the service we find prayer that the Holy
Spirit may continue to be active in the lives of those who were
received into the Church by baptism. The promises have
given expression to the candidates' own confirmation of their
place in the Church; the emphasis now, quite rightly, is on the
confirming work of God.

The societary element in Methodism, with its emphasis
upon 'membership', makes its presence felt in the words of
welcome which follow:

We welcome you into the full membership of the Christian
Church and the Society in this place.[30]

Despite the inevitable confusion caused by the term 'full
membership', the 1974 service is much more successful than
that of 1936 in showing the relationship between baptism and
confirmation and in linking both to the Christian's personal
development. The two liturgical acts, infant baptism and confirmation, which Methodism normally uses for initiation are,
therefore, quite compatible with the theology of initiation as
we have set it out in Chapters Three and Four.

**The Baptism of those who are able to answer for themselves,
with the Public Reception into Full Membership, or
Confirmation**
This is the form of service with which, presumably, the early
Church would have felt most at home, though it is rarely
required today. It is intended, of course, for previously
unbaptized believers, and as such it is able to exploit to the full
the rich baptismal imagery of the New Testament.

It is not necessary for us to examine the rite with the same

[29] Ibid., p.A23
[30] Ibid., p.A24

attention to detail which we devoted to the other initiation services, for there is no dispute about the appropriateness of this form of baptism for the incorporation into the Church of adult converts or of those who, desiring to be full members of the Church, find that they are unbaptized. Infant baptism and confirmation are surrounded by controversy; believers' baptism *in the circumstances which we have described* is not. It is worth noting, however, that this service is much less restrained than the service of infant baptism in its references to cleansing and to regeneration. Cleansing is suggested by the opening sentence of the Old Testament lesson (Ezekiel 36:25–28):

> I will sprinkle clean water upon you, and you shall be clean from all your uncleannesses.[31]

The concept re-appears in the hymn between the Epistle and the Gospel:

> O that the souls baptized therein
>   May now thy truth and mercy feel;
> May rise and wash away their sin;
>   Come, Holy Ghost, their pardon seal.[32]

There is, of course, no difficulty here as there is in infant baptism. No sensible Christian doubts the existence of actual sin; but original sin is a much less widely accepted doctrine. Regeneration is introduced in the Gospel (John 3:1–7) which tells of Jesus's conversation with Nicodemus about 'being born of water and the Spirit', and the baptismal prayer takes up the theme:

> . . . We pray that they who are now to be baptized in this water, having professed their faith in Christ, and being born again of the Spirit, may die to sin and be raised to the new life of righteousness in Christ.[33]

It is not clear, however, whether rebirth is here thought to

[31] Ibid., p.A30
[32] Ibid., p.A32
[33] Ibid., p.A34

precede baptism or to accompany it. Perhaps this ambiguity is to be welcomed: the important point is that birth marks a beginning, as baptism marks a beginning, and that ongoing Christian development is vital. In this connection, it is also noteworthy that the congregation is asked to give a promise, similar to that given in infant baptism,[34] to maintain the common life of worship and service so that the baptized may grow in grace, knowledge and love. The service thus rightly points out that post-baptismal growth is not the monopoly of infants.

This chapter completes our investigation into the history and theology of infant baptism and related rites. We have made out a case to the effect that baptism can be administered to infants without doing violence to the New Testament doctrine of baptism; we have sought to apply this understanding of infant baptism to the process of development in Christian discipleship; and we have tried to demonstrate that the recently authorized initiation services of Methodism give expression, by and large, to the theological stance which we have taken.

A further task now lies ahead of us, for the baptismal controversies of the late twentieth century are occasioned at least as much by practical considerations as by differences of theological opinion. In modern Western society, often said to be post-Christian, which infants ought to be baptized? How are ministers to set about preparing parents for their important role in baptism? Is a strict baptismal policy necessary? Or should infant baptism be replaced by some other sort of service? Part Two will examine the issues raised by questions such as these.

[34] See above, p.93

PART TWO
Baptism in Practice

CHAPTER SIX

Christian Parents?

'THE CHILDREN of Christian parents are brought to be baptized . . .'[1] At the end of Chapter Three,[2] we suggested that the theological case for infant baptism which we presented in that chapter depends upon the assumption that the parents who present their children for baptism will be practising Christians. Without being unduly selective in the use of New Testament theology it is impossible to justify totally indiscriminate baptism, and the Church has always assumed that parents who presented their children were in fact Christians. The nature of modern society, however, raises serious doubts about this assumption. According to Geoffrey Wainright,

> the empirical fact is that there are at the moment millions of baptized persons, baptized years ago in infancy, who have not the faintest existential notion of the worship, fellowship, service and mission involved in the Christian life; and the denominations of today add to their future number by continuing to baptize as infants people who stand perhaps even less chance of coming to personal commitment.[3]

Though the demand for Christian baptism is gradually declining, it is still true that every year a large number of parents

[1] *M.S.B.*, p.A7. See above, pp.90f.
[2] See above, pp.66f.
[3] Wainright, op. cit., p.72

present their children for baptism and that the number of baptized children who subsequently lapse is considerable. In 1956, there were 602 baptisms in the Church of England per thousand live births, and though there is no means of knowing how many of their parents were then actively involved in the Church or how many of the babies then baptized are now themselves practising Christians, it is obvious enough that nowhere near 60 per cent of Britain's 22 or 23–year-olds are still actively involved with the Church of England.Ten per cent would be a more than optimistic estimate. If baptism is the beginning of the Christian life, it seems that it is also, for the great majority of the baptized, the last stage of involvement with the Church.

Many people find this situation acutely disturbing, though the high fall-out rate can be variously interpreted. Some would argue that the children of practising Christians are just as likely to drift away from the Church as those whose parents are not practising Christians; and it is undoubtedly true that not all children of practising Christians proceed to confirmation and that, of those who do, many leave the Church subsequently. But others would maintain that there is infinitely more likelihood of growth towards commitment in the case of children whose parents are deeply involved in the life of the Church. The argument, which cannot easily be refuted, is that infant baptism is extremely unlikely to lead towards a mature understanding of and participation in the Christian life for a child whose parents do not attach any importance to belonging to the Church and who therefore receives no Christian teaching (except, perhaps, for one hour per week at Sunday school), has none of the advantages of a Christian environment in the home, and who is not encouraged in any way to look to the Christian community for nurture. In other words, baptism divorced from the environment in which its meaning can be understood and appropriated by the baptized is so incomplete as to be without existential significance to the individual. 'There is no benefit in baptism out of the context of churchmanship',[4] for the baptized is given no opportunity to grow into what he is. This is not a new situation. As long ago as 1940, Alec Vidler lamented the fact that

[4] Alec R. Vidler in *Theology*, July 1940, p.6

as a matter of course we baptize children who are born into households which even the most brazen latitudinarian would hesitate to call Christian.[5]

The remaining chapters of this book are largely concerned with the question, what should the Church's response be to those parents, who are not practising Christians, but who wish to have their children baptized? And, in the light of what we have already said, we must be aware that we are discussing the Church's attitude towards the overwhelming majority of parents.

What prompts parents who are not practising Christians to ask for the baptism of their offspring? The question is peculiarly modern. It would have been impossible to ask it during the first three centuries of Christianity's existence, when the Church was a persecuted minority. No one who was not a practising Christian or a new convert to Christianity would have any reason to seek baptism for his child. From the time of Constantine onwards, the question would have been equally inappropriate, for during the centuries of Christendom's existence, the ideas that being a Christian was a matter of choice or that anyone should fail to present his children for the sacrament of baptism were unthinkable. If one was a Frenchman or an Englishman or an Italian one was a Christian and one had become a Christian at baptism. It is, of course, true that during these long centuries there must have been very many baptized 'Christians' whose religious belief was minimal and whose religious observance was insincere and perfunctory but who, from fear of persecution or of the contempt of their neighbours, could not admit that the official religion meant little or nothing to them. It is one of the scandals of history that a Christian society should have created such a state of affairs; but it is a fact that a person was believed to be a Christian by virtue of his baptism and that baptism was universal.

In the nineteenth and twentieth centuries irresistible forces have effectively destroyed this notion of an automatic connection between nationality and religion. Powerful trades unions put an end to the objectionable practices of those

[5] Ibid., p.3

northern mill-owners who enticed working people into their own churches and chapels as a condition of employment and kept them there by threat of dismissal. Universal education taught people to think freely and free thought often led to rejection of the fundamentalist Christianity of the chapel sermon and the Sunday school lesson. The bitter experience of war not only posed deep questions about the reality of a God of love but also removed people from a home environment in which church-going was part of the accepted lifestyle. The growth of the entertainment industry, especially in cinema, radio, television, bingo, Sunday sport, 'pop' culture and the 'family pub', provided exciting options to people whose social life had previously centred on the concerts and outings of the local church. No one could now be forced into belonging to the Church, and thousands who found its doctrines untenable or its social life inadequate ceased to belong. A post-Christian society was born.

Yet this is not the whole story. For, as we have said, a great many of the people who, consciously or unconsciously, have liberated themselves from active involvement in church life still ask for their children to be baptized. This may mean that such people have a vestigial sense of belonging to the Church, a phenomenon which interests sociologists of religion:

> The empty pews of every church are 'filled' by people who identify themselves with a particular denomination, or in a local community with an actual building, even though the pews remain empty. The vast majority of the population still identify themselves with a particular denomination.[6]

A. Raymond George, therefore, is surely right in concluding that:

> Society is now more aptly described as post-Christian than as Christian; but the word 'pagan', which some writers use, completely fails to understand it.[7]

For there is an important difference between a society which

---

[6] John S. Lampard, *Look at your Church,* Epworth Press, 1975, p.76
[7] A. Raymond George in *Epworth Review,* May 1977, pp.61f. (This article is cited hereafter as George, *ER.*)

was once Christian and one which was never Christian; and Britain is an example of the former, in which Christian ideas and values and especially 'life rituals', such as baptism, marriage and burial, have made a deep impression on national life and have somehow penetrated the recesses of the minds of people who have rejected, or never experienced, the practice of institutional religion.

It is difficult to know how to describe these people whose link with the ongoing life of the Church is at best tenuous yet who nevertheless feel that they belong to it in some sense. And there is little doubt that the description which we apply to them tends to colour our judgment about their suitability as parents to present their children for baptism. It is easier to accept 'nominal Christians' than 'pagans', harder to accommodate 'non-Christians' than 'lapsed Christians'. George is surely correct in dismissing the word 'pagan' as entirely inappropriate, and he may also be right in suggesting that 'non-Christians', a term which the present writer has previously used,[8] is too negative.[9] After all, most of the parents involved are baptized, and this fact, supported by their desire to avail their offspring of the rite of baptism, suggests that they have a religion, whether or not they practise it. George prefers 'nominal Christians' or 'lapsed Christians', both of which are fairly accurate terms, thought it may be felt that the former at least is too positive, unless the emphasis is placed very firmly on the adjective. The history of the word 'lapsed' in Christian usage implies a greater degree of commitment in the past than many nominal Christians may have had. It seems best, on the whole, to refer to 'parents who are not practising Christians' or 'non-practising Christians', for these are straightforward descriptive expressions which do not suffer from the disadvantages which, as we have seen, other terms entail.

Some writers place great emphasis upon the presumed Christianity of such parents. In a major defence of what he calls 'general' baptism, R. R. Osborn[10] argues that the concept of Christendom has deeply affected and continues to

---

[8] Neil Dixon, *Epworth Review,* January 1977, pp.7–12 (cited hereafter as Dixon, *ER.)*
[9] George, *ER,* p.62
[10] R. R. Osborn, *Forbid Them Not,* S.P.C.K., 1972

affect the national life socially and ethically and that 'general' baptism has been significantly instrumental in this:

> When Otto declared thirty years ago that 'England is still the most religious country in Europe', he explained to Dean Matthews that he meant 'that England is the one country in Europe in which large sections of the population are guided in public and private affairs by Christian principles'. Quite so. The explanation lies deep in English history, and the link between behaviour and belief lies ultimately in the fact that most Englishmen have been baptized in infancy.[11]

In the light of what we have already said[12] about the relationship between Church and society in modern Britain, it may well be thought that Osborn's assessment is unduly optimistic. But Osborn regards the continuing demand for infant baptism as an important indication that the Christendom concept is still very much alive:

> Is it not . . . a very important point that this service is being voluntarily asked for? There is no compulsion about baptism; no one forces parents to have children baptized . . . Baptism is freely asked for and—even when delayed for one of many reasons, good or bad, grave or trivial—eagerly sought. To seek to alter this position, on grounds of principle, is to move into an area where 'A bruised reed he shall not break, and the smoking flax he shall not quench' has been written for our admonition.[13]

Similarly George writes:

> The extent of their lapse may be greater than in earlier times, but their very desire to have their children baptized shows that it is not complete.[14]

This brings us back to the question which sparked off our discussion of non-practising Christians and the nature of modern society. What is it that prompts parents who are not practising Christians to request the baptism of their offspring? We have already mentioned the vestigial sense of

[11] Ibid., p.6
[12] See above, pp.105ff.
[13] Osborn, op. cit., p.2
[14] George, *E.R.*, p.62

belonging experienced by some parents. In these cases there tends to be a strong conviction that the administration of baptism is not merely desirable but essential. It is 'the right thing to do' to have the baby baptized. This conviction is surely no less real because many parents cannot offer any explanation for it.

But sometimes discussion reveals that the vestigial belief and sense of belonging are not the parents' but the grandparents' or those of other influential relations or friends. In such instances parents who are not themselves convinced of the necessity of baptism may request it in order to keep the peace within their family or circle of friends. Superstition may also lead non-practising Christians to request a child's baptism. Most ministers have encountered such superstitition in one form or another, though many church-members may not be aware how widespread it is. The following quotations are a sample of superstitious statements made to ministers within the last four or five years:

> In our family we believe in having them christened as soon as possible. They thrive better afterwards.

> The hole in the head closes up when they're 'done'.

> If they've been christened, they're not as likely to get measles.

> My wife can't use the carving knife until the baby's been christened.

> If you won't christen it, it'll never be able to see its grandma. She won't let it into her house until it's been done; and she won't come to our house either.

The superstitious desire to fend off measles, to close up the imagined hole in the head, or to allow mother and child to visit grandmother without fear of calamitous consequences is, it need hardly be said, totally irreconcilable with the Christian understanding of baptism. The extent to which such notions survive, even among young parents, in our modern 'technological' society is both surprising and alarming. It may well be a more important motive than is often realized in encouraging parents who are not practising Christians to seek their infants' baptism.

Other parents say that they want their child to have God's blessing. It is often exceedingly difficult for a minister to draw out precisely what is meant by this expression, but there seems to be a vague underlying concept of God withholding his blessing from unbaptized children but bestowing it bountifully as a result of baptism. Baptism is necessary to put a child in God's 'good books'; it ensures that God will take care of the child. Without baptism a child is impoverished, if not endangered. This doctrine is not significantly different from overt superstition.

An apparently more congenial reason for wanting their infants baptized is given by some parents who maintain that they want their child to have a Christian upbringing from the outset. This is often said by non-practising Christian parents without any sense of incongruity on their part. They declare that they intend to admit the child to Sunday school at the earliest opportunity, as they themselves were probably admitted, so that he may learn 'all about religion'. The fact that they are not themselves involved in the life of the Church does not seem to them relevant in any way, for on their own terms they are Christians. Many will say that they believe in God and try to lead good lives and that, for them, these things constitute Christianity. 'You can be a Christian without going to church.'

This quotation brings us to what is perhaps the heart of the contemporary problem. For there is undoubtedly a dichotomy between the Church's understanding of what it means to be a Christian and that of the community at large.[15] The difficulty is partly linguistic. 'Christian' has come to have a very vague meaning in common parlance, often more or less synonymous with 'good'. A man who performs a kindly deed may well be told that he has done a Christian act (or, if he behaves unkindly, that he is unChristian), quite regardless of any profession of faith. He may be a Jew or a Muslim or a Buddhist or an atheist, but his deed is still described as Christian. This linguistic imprecision reflects a widespread notion

[15] It is, however, true that a good many churchgoers also subscribe to the view that 'you can be a Christian without going to church'

that to be a Christian is to be a decent sort of person, obeying the law of the land (within reason), giving other people an occasional helping hand, and (though this is desirable rather than essential) believing in God. But going to church, reading the Bible or talking about Jesus Christ are hobbies for those who like doing such things. They are not necessary. One can easily be a Christian without them.

It is, of course, true that many people who think in this way are also sympathetic to the Church and its activities without wishing to be too closely involved in them. In 1973, 90 per cent of the residents of a small northern town asserted in a survey that they would regret the fact if there were no churches in the place. Financial appeals for the restoration of church buildings usually elicit a generous response from people who hardly ever use them. And those who say that 'you can be a Christian without going to church' are glad enough to come to church for the 'life rituals'. Many adults think that Sunday schools provide good moral grounding for children, which will equip them to be respectable, decent (nominal) Christians like their parents.

Added to all this, and perhaps implied by most of it, is innate conservatism. Having a baby baptized seems to many people to be the natural thing to do, and they are surprised when anyone, especially a minister, questions them about their motives. Some indeed think that they have a *legal* rite to have their child baptized.[16] In view of the strong emphasis which the Church itself has traditionally placed on the duty of parents to present their children for baptism, it is hardly surprising that many parents still feel that this is the right thing for them to do, however confused and (from a theological point of view) inadequate their motives might be. As Vidler says, 'it is not the parents who are to blame for the present state of affairs. The whole Church, and not least the clergy themselves, are to blame'.[17]

In summarizing what we have said in this chapter, it is important that we should try to describe more succinctly the

[16] It is often said that every Englishman has a legal right to have his offspring baptized in the Church of England; but Colin Buchanan has demonstrated that this statement is indefensible. See Buchanan, *Discipline,* p.12
[17] Vidler, op. cit., p.8

nature of the society in which we live and the implications of that description for infant baptism. We may most easily approach this description by first saying what modern society is not.

First, present day society is not dominated by practising Christians. Communicant members of the churches represent only a small percentage of the population in general and of the parents who present their children for baptism in particular. Only about 15 per cent of the population regularly attend church.[18]

But, second, twentieth-century society is not to be described as pagan. We often talk rather loosely about a 'missionary situation', but it is necessary to draw a distinction between a country where the gospel is preached for the first time, where converts are made and baptized as believers, and a country in which Christian beliefs and practices have influenced people's thinking over a long period of time, however casually the mass of the population may treat religious observances. If we *are* in a missionary situation, it is quite different from the traditional concept of such a situation. There is, in British society, an underlying though largely dormant Christian tradition, far removed indeed from commitment to Christ and his Church, which is nevertheless influential. Many people who never go near a church feel that, in some sense, they belong to one. There is general sympathy for the Church and a feeling among many people that they are Christians.[19]

The early Church was not faced with this state of affairs, nor, in the early days of missionary expansion, were the 'young' churches of more recent times. In those eras, a person either belonged to the Church, in that he believed its doctrines, shared in its worship, and made his own contribution to its corporate life, or he stood firmly outside it. Nor is our present situation comparable with the centuries during which the concept of a national religion was still tenable. Our circumstances are historically unique.

In these circumstances, the Church is frequently confronted by parents who are perhaps themselves baptized, who believe they have some sort of association with the Church,

[18] Lampard, op. cit., p.77
[19] See Lampard, op. cit., pp.73–9

who may believe in God and consider themselves to be Christians, yet who have no personal commitment to Jesus Christ, who rarely if ever worship, and who have no real contact with any local church. Can the Church accept them on their own estimate as 'Christian parents', entitled to present their children for Christian baptism?

> Election lies ultimately in the mysterious will of God, and baptism and non-baptism are no final guarantee of salvation and damnation respectively: but it would be clean contrary to the New Testament to pretend that there was meant to be anything but a very close correspondence, if not identity, between the baptized and the truly Christian. If the Church is to be a faithful steward of the divine sacraments, then it must consider carefully the question of who shall be given baptism.[20]

[20] Wainwright, op. cit., p. 72

CHAPTER SEVEN

Preparation and Instruction

In 1974, after leaving theological college, a young minister arrived in a certain circuit to take up his first appointment. In college he had often taken part in discussions about infant baptism, but had never doubted its validity or recognized the existence of any practical difficulties associated with it. For two reasons, however, he was to become very worried about the whole issue. First, the area was intensely superstitious, with more than its share of people who believed that an unbaptized child could not be taken out of his home and so on, with the result that there was an unusually high demand for baptism. Second, it was customary for baptisms to be administered without the parents being prepared or instructed in any way; indeed, most baptisms were arranged by an insurance agent, a member of the church, who would write down the names of persons desiring their children's baptism, tell them to come to church at a certain time, and pass on the information to the minister, who was expected to be in church at the right time to perform the baptisms. (A few years before this, the minister was to learn, there had been an even worse situation: the insurance agent had not only made all the arrangements, but he had actually administered baptism himself!)

There is no evidence to suggest that this story, recounted to the present writer by the minister involved, is typical of Methodist churches in general, though some ministers are prepared to confess that, weary of trying to do more or believing that more is unnecessary, they limit their pre-baptismal interview with parents to obtaining the necessary details and fixing a date for the baptism. Most ministers, however, seem to take seriously the Church's rules about instruction:

> As soon as possible after notice has been given, full enquiry should be made and all necessary instruction and exposition of the service given by the minister, a deaconess, or some other competent and instructed leader. For this purpose the parents or guardians may be visited in their home, or they should be asked to attend at the church at a convenient hour. Instruction should be regarded as particularly necessary in the case of a first child, or of the first baptism from the home according to the Methodist rite.[1]

Before the Interview
Some ministers have found it helpful to give parents a written document as soon as the request for baptism is received and before any interview takes place. In some cases the document is intended to give a brief exposition of the meaning of baptism and of the duties of parents; in others its purpose is to make plain the procedure of the local church in respect of baptisms. Hundreds of these locally-produced documents must be in circulation: we shall quote from three of them in this chapter. The first is the most pungent:

> Dear parents,
> I am writing to you so that you may think carefully about the meaning of baptism before proceeding any further.
> *What is baptism?* Baptism is the ancient service of the Church that marks entry into the Church. Originally baptism followed conversion to the Christian faith.
> *Why infant baptism?* Children should not be excluded from the Christian Church. If their parents are practising Christians it is right to baptize the children, and this has been the custom from the earliest days of the Church.
> *What is expected of parents whose children are baptized?*
> Three questions are asked of parents:
> 'Will you provide for this your child a Christian home of love and faithfulness?'
> 'Will you help him by your words, prayers and example to renounce all evil and to put his trust in Jesus Christ his Saviour?'
> 'Will you encourage him to enter into the full membership of the Church, and to serve Christ in the world?'
> In a nutshell this is asking both of you to make a public

[1] *M.S.B.*, p. A2f.

profession of Christian faith and to put it bluntly we do not expect you to lie about it. If you have answered the above questions 'yes' we shall think it strange if we do not see you in church regularly. Make no mistake about it, that is the lowest possible interpretation of the questions and answers.

If you are not happy about the above, ask yourself why you want to present your child for baptism—to have a family party?—to follow social conventions? There is nothing magical about baptism. It will not make your child grow any better, or faster. If your child is not baptized it will not remove him from the love of God. Remember baptism is about membership of the Christian Church.

Yours sincerely

It may be felt that this letter is unduly provocative in its use of such phrases as 'why do you want to present your child for baptism?—to have a family party?—to follow social conventions?' and 'we do not expect you to lie about it'. The minister who wrote it and uses it, however, explains the circumstances of its conception:

> Before I moved to . . . I had already decided to make use of some such letter, but when I arrived here I found that the local rector was also pursuing a similar policy. This resulted in a positive deluge of requests for baptism (in the Methodist church). My predecessor had baptized more or less indiscriminately and this had meant a baptism at virtually every morning service when he was preaching and a very perturbed church.
>
> My policy has not been without its problems. Some of my people do not approve, and some parents have been abusive ('What right have you. . . ?'). Some of the subsequent interviews have been very difficult. The great majority of parents to whom I have sent my letter do not then ask for an interview (that in itself has saved a great deal of time). Three or four couples have started attending church and every baptism has been meaningful. (The rector tells me that his policy has been similarly successful.)

Two points, one positive, the other negative, should be noted. First, a few of the parents who have received this letter have been challenged to such an extent that they have started attending worship. But second, the majority of parents were dissuaded by it from pursuing the matter further and some were made angry by it. In Chapter Eight we shall examine further the issues raised by these points. Is it true that a rigorous policy produces good results? Is the Church ever right to antagonize parents or dissuade them from presenting their children for baptism?

The second document is used by all the ministers in a certain circuit:

Your child and baptism: The Methodist Church
The Methodist Church requires that before a baptism is arranged there must be an interview with the minister or other responsible person. These notes are written to help any questions you may have. You can then discuss some of these points with the minister.

What is baptism? Baptism is entry into the Christian Church and the pledge to become followers of Jesus Christ. It is not therefore a mere social occasion but a specifically Christian act—we call it a 'sacrament' which means it is a way of conveying God's love to us.

Why do we baptize children? The Methodist Church does, though not all churches do. We believe that for the children of Christian parents it is right to declare the way in which God loves them even before they are able to respond consciously to it. The order of service puts it this way: '. . . the children of Christian parents are brought to be baptized with water as a sign of the new life in Christ, and to be made members of God's family the Church.' But a child cannot understand this. So, the parents have an important part to play. They undertake promises on the child's behalf. This means that when the child is old enough to respond to them personally it is right to become a member of the Church through the service of confirmation. What happens in baptism is brought to completion in confirmation.

What are these promises? There are three. You must promise (1) 'To provide for this child a Christian home of love and faithfulness'. (2) 'To help him by your words, prayers and example to renounce all evil and to put his trust in Jesus Christ his Saviour'. (3) 'To encourage him to enter into the full membership of the Church, and to serve Christ in the world.' These are very serious promises and not to be made lightly. They ask questions of your own faith and life. If you make them, it implies that you yourselves have an active Christian faith.

Does that mean we have to come to church? We do not refuse to baptize an infant simply because the parents do not come to church. At the same time it could be said that your regular attendance at worship would be a proof that you really mean the promises.

Isn't all this the duty of godparents? The Methodist Church does not insist on having godparents. We do in some churches have 'sponsors'. These are chosen, one by the parents, and one by the minister from among the congregation. They make the promise to 'support these parents in the Christian upbringing of this child'. So it is obviously appropriate that any sponsors should be practising Christians. Nevertheless, it is the parents who bear the final responsibility before God for the Christian upbringing of the child.

Shouldn't religion be left for the child to decide? Since it is a personal commitment, it has to be. However, if you believe it should be left, without influence from you, until the child is old enough to make up his own mind then infant baptism is not what you are looking for. The promises you make state clearly that you will bring up the child believing the Christian faith and having a personal trust in Jesus Christ his Saviour.

What if I can't make those promises? The child will not come to any harm by not being baptized (in spite of any superstitions you might have heard). It is becoming increasingly common for people to be baptized when they come to a personal faith in later years. But it is still possible for your child to be dedicated.

What is dedication? A form of service in which we thank God for the gift of the child and dedicate him to God. Prayers are offered for the child, for his home, family, and those who will have care of him. It is not a kind of second-class baptism. It is something quite different: being thankful to God. If you do not feel able to take the baptismal promises honestly, then this may be the appropriate way forward.

Can't we have a quiet baptism on our own? No. The Methodist Church requires that, except in situations of the gravest emergency, the baptism shall take place in public worship, and both parents shall be present. The normal congregation is required to receive the child. This means the baptism will take place at whatever time your local church has its services.

What should I do next? If when you have read this paper carefully you discuss it amongst yourselves you may then like to raise some of these points when you see the minister. Then it should be easier for you to reach your decision.

This document, also used as a preliminary to an interview, is far more pacific in tone than the one which we considered first, yet, says its author:

it has resulted in several people saying that they will not proceed further with the matter. All this document in fact does is to draw out the present baptismal policy of Methodism from the Conference statement and the rubrics of the actual service.

Here again, we observe that parents can be dissuaded by such a document. We also notice that a service of dedication, as opposed to baptism, is suggested as a possible alternative. This is another issue which we must consider, and we shall do so in Chapter Nine.

Our third document was drawn up by a minister in a small town a few years ago and was subsequently adopted, with a few necessary modifications, by the Anglican priest in the parish:

> In order that both the parents and the godparents of babies to be baptized in . . . Methodist Church may fully understand the purpose and significance of Christian baptism, and the importance of the promises which they themselves are asked to make at baptism, those who wish to have a child baptized will be asked to agree to the following:
> (i)   To select as godparents people who are practising Christians (i.e. active members of a Christian Church). If this is difficult to arrange, either (a) the minister may himself appoint godparents or (b) godparents may at his discretion be dispensed with.
> (ii) To attend a meeting with the minister, at a time to be mutually agreed, at which both the parents and all the godparents are present to discuss with the minister the meaning of baptism and the importance of the baptismal promises.
> (iii) To attend a rehearsal of the service at the church on the Saturday evening immediately preceding the baptism, together with the godparents.

After this statement, the document requests parents to supply details of names, the child's date of birth, and so on, including the names of proposed godparents and the churches of which they are members. Parents are also required to give an undertaking that they will comply with the church's requirements. This differs from the two other documents cited in that it makes no attempt to discuss the theology of baptism or the significance of the promises, but sets out the discipline of the local church in respect of sponsors, interviews and rehearsals. The minister who devised the system says:

> The document was fully discussed, and eventually approved, by the Leaders' Meeting. Some members of the meeting felt that it might deter some parents, though others, including me, thought that this would be no bad thing! In the event, I was very surprised to discover that only one couple who had approached me failed to return the form and request an interview.
>
> Apart from the serious lack of understanding about baptism among parents, the biggest difficulty has been in the matter of sponsors. It will be noticed that I dared to deviate from the officially recommended practice of having two sponsors, one appointed by the parents and the other by the minister, which seems to me quite impracticable. The reason for insisting that the godparents should be practising Christians was that there is absolutely no justification for godparents who are not. But I have had grave doubts about the *bona fides* of many of those who have been appointed.

It is interesting to observe that this document, unlike the others, did not deter parents from proceeding, perhaps because it reserved discussion of the theology of baptism and the duties of parents for the subsequent interview. The other issue raised above, that of godparents, will be considered in Chapter Eight.

This small sample of written material illustrates the way in which three ministers have attempted to prepare the ground for the interview which the Church requires, and to which we now turn our attention.

The Interview
It is often said that an interview with parents who are seeking a child's baptism presents a minister with a splendid opportunity to instruct people in the basic elements of the Christian faith and to call for a response. Here is a ready-made situation of contact between a minister and a couple of young adults who are not practising Christians. The Church is always eager, surely, to make such contacts; what an excellent evangelistic opportunity this occasion provides. But this line of reasoning depends upon assumptions that are questionable:

The majority of practical experiments imply that their authors believe Britain to be still enough of a Christian country for the baptismal problem to be treated as *pastoral* rather than *strictly missionary*. By this I mean that their approach is designed to *recall* to lapsed parents *the faith which they are already supposed to know*. The baptism of an infant is made the opportunity for teaching the parents more about the meaning of their own baptism, in the hope that they may be recalled to a living faith and bring up their children in the Christian way.[2]

It will be argued, however, that such estimates of the potential effectiveness of interviews are inflated. Most of the instances where baptismal interviews lead to real Christian commitment on the part of parents appear to occur in the context of a rigorous baptismal policy.[3] But often interviews involve interesting and enjoyable discussions, especially when the parents are articulate, at the end of which two clear points of view will have been expressed but nothing will have been settled.

Take the question, 'Will you provide for this your child a Christian home of love and faithfulness?'. Time and again, when asked what in their estimation this question means, parents will answer to this effect: 'A good, loving home'. If the minister attempts, as he surely must, to present the idea that something more specific is intended by the words 'Christian home', in that acceptance of the Person and authority of Christ and belonging to the Christian community are implied, he is likely to be met with a familiar argument: 'You can be a Christian without going to church'. A lengthy debate about this contentious statement will perhaps be interesting; but at the end of it, as likely as not, both sides will be sticking to their guns.[4]

Some ministers confess that they conduct interviews by expounding the Christian doctrine of baptism and the responsibilities of parents in the form of a monologue. This approach assumes that the parents are really interested in knowing what baptism is all about—an assumption which is not unreasonable considering that they have requested the

[2] Wainwright, op. cit., p.76
[3] See below, pp.134–138
[4] Dixon, *E.R.*, p.9

sacrament for their child. But are they really interested? There seem to be many parents who, for one reason or another, desire the baptism of their child, but want it to take place with as little fuss as possible. The interview seems to them a burdensome preliminary which it is necessary for them to endure in order to secure the baptism. It would be a grave mistake to think that such parents are sitting on the edges of their seats, anxious to take in every word of baptismal theology that issues from the minister's mouth. The impression is often given that they simply want the minister to fix the date, stop talking, and go home. One minister recalls a visit during which the infant's father continued to glance furtively at the television screen (the sound had been turned down but the picture remained) throughout the interview, and displayed absolutely no interest in discussing the question of baptism. Another minister describes his experiences of interviewing parents in 'an exceedingly conservative place, full of traditions and superstitions', where he was 'inundated with requests from people of every kind':

> Ignorance and aggression when a request was not immediately and unconditionally granted caused me to think hard. What was baptism? I tried hard to teach the party line. Many of the parents just nodded, but clearly understood little or nothing of what I was saying, unless I made myself almost objectionable; in which case the response was 'You mean that you won't do it?'. All I wanted was conscientious and thoughtful participation in the vows and some assurance of follow-up—in other words that the sacrament should be a sacrament, and not just a performance of social ritual.

There seem to be four principal difficulties about baptismal interviews: First, many parents start off with the assumption that their child has a *right* to be baptized, and consider that any discussion of the matter is unnecessary. This leads some of them to become angry or abusive, a phenomenon described by several ministers. For example,

> In the course of what I hope was kindly interviewing, I have uncovered some interesting reactions. It is not uncommon when I pose the question, 'Now why do you want your child baptized?' to meet with the response 'Because I do, and that's that'.

One mother said to me, 'If you don't christen this child and anything happens to her, it'll be your fault. You'll be for it then, my lad.'

Another minister recounts an almost incredible story. A young serviceman telephoned him about the baptism of his baby. The minister began to explain that an interview would be necessary and made reference to the church in which the child would be baptized. The serviceman impatiently interrupted him: 'Why do we have to have all that fuss. Can't you just come round to the house and do him over the kitchen sink?' When his request was refused, he became abusive and slammed his telephone receiver down.

Second, many parents are not in the least interested in Christian beliefs and simply do not want to know what the baptismal service means, though they are unlikely to admit it in so many words. They have their own (often superstitious and usually quite inadequate) understanding of the rite and are resistant to hearing the Church's teaching expounded. This creates a most unsatisfactory climate for discussion.

Third, many parents are quite content to let the minister say what he feels must be said and to acquiesce in what he says. Sometimes they will promise to attend church in future, even without any solicitation of this promise by the minister. A minister quoted above referred to parents who 'just nodded, but clearly understood little or nothing of what I was saying', and as Ian Yates wrote a few years ago:

> If parents have decided that they want their child baptized then they will give all the 'right' answers and there is no way of telling whether they really mean what they say or not.[5]

Fourth, many articulate parents who enjoy a lively discussion will enter into the spirit of the debate but will not waver from their own rather humanistic interpretation of what being a Christian means. This leaves the minister in a position where he has to decide whether he can allow the promises to be made on an understanding of their meaning which is different from his own or whether he ought to refuse the baptism. With

[5] The *Methodist Recorder*, 3 May, 1973

all these problems in mind, let us look at one minister's account of his experiences with interviews. Like some other ministers, he prefers to meet parents in groups. This seems to be a helpful method in churches where there are sufficient requests for baptism to make it possible.

Sometimes with Bibles, in a group of parents, we look at the primary examples of baptism in the New Testament. Baptism is a sign of what has happened—repentance, faith, becoming one of God's new covenant people. I point out that this is as far as the Baptists go, but that Methodists look at the very few but significant cases of 'family baptisms' where whole families were baptized. We also look at the healing stories where wholeness (salvation) comes through the faith not of the person who was ill, but the persons who carried him, or his father or master. So faith is seen as something not co-terminous with our skin boundary. 'Family baptism' can be administered if the elements of repentance, faith, incorporation into the Church are present in the family, and mainly exercised by the parents in the family and the congregation. 'Family baptism' is a sacrament because it is a sign of what has happened—i.e. the child is living in a Christian family, with all that involves, and the whole family is in the fellowship of the Church.

I then turn to the *Entry into the Church* booklet and describe it as one service of initiation separated into two parts for members of Christian families. The 'family baptism' comes first, where repentance and faith are present, the faith being that of one or both parents and of their congregation, the new life of salvation being that of the Christian family and the local congregation. The second part is confirmation and reception into full membership where the repentance and faith are those of the grown-up baby, and the new life is his own personal life and the life of the congregation that welcomes him. I turn to page A7 of my *Methodist Service Book* and point out the phrase, 'Thus the children of Christian parents . . .' and say that the Methodist position on 'family baptism' is that at least one parent is Christian.

At about this stage, if not before for perceptive parents, they voice the question 'Do you mean that you are going to baptize my baby only if we go to your church?' We can then have a talk about 'going to your church' or 'belonging to our church'. The other type of objection is based on 'the divine right of every child to be baptized' which many fringe Christians seem to believe in quite genuinely. They also talk about the children being deprived if they are not baptized or feeling disappointed when they learn, years later, that they weren't 'done' as babies.

My reply generally is that there is no divine right for babies to be baptized. Obviously if the parents were Muslim or animist and thought that Christian baptism would be a nice extra, we should refuse. I say that I don't think God loves any child the less for the lack of a cup or bath full of water. The deprivation comes not from the lack of water but the lack of Christian family and congregational life which brings God's grace in a specific way to the child. To the argument of being disappointed, I say that the real disappointment for them would be to become committed Christians and then realize that they had the outward sign of 'family baptism' but that there was no family faith and Christian life to give that sign some meaning, as their parents were not ready for 'family baptism'.

In all these sorts of cases, I hasten to add that I am not refusing to baptize their child, but that the important thing to do is to help the parents to express the faith that they say they have. When we have helped them to express their faith in the local congregation's life, then the conditions hold which make baptism a reality. I offer them more visits, Bible discussions, involvement in various groups to help them feel that they belong.

The result: some people do not contact me again. Some get very angry. With some I end up by saying that I don't think they want for their child what the Methodist Church means by baptism, and that they should look round for a church that will just 'do' a child with no questions asked.

Opinions will vary about the extent to which the theology of baptism, as expounded to parents by this minister, is satisfactory; but our quotation makes one thing very clear. The business of trying to urge upon parents who are not practising Christians the commitment which their promises will imply is fraught with difficulties.

In this chapter we have examined some of the complex issues involved in dealing with parents of this sort, at a small sample of pre-interview literature, and at some of the problems related to interviews themselves. We have seen that there are many instances of interviews not solving problems but rather creating further difficulties. That 'splendid evangelistic opportunity' is often a highly unsatisfactory confrontation which leaves parents angry and confused and ministers perplexed.

CHAPTER EIGHT

The Crisis

JEREMIAS tells us that 'in the fourth century there occurred a great crisis in the matter of infant baptism',[1] by which he means the widespread tendency to postpone baptism for fear of the consequences of post-baptismal sin. Has another crisis occurred in the twentieth century? Certainly the higher courts of the denominations do not appear to regard the present unease about infant baptism as critical; but there are many ministers and some laymen who find themselves involved in difficulties about the practice which they regard as crisis situations. This chapter will draw together some of the questions raised by Chapters Six and Seven and suggest some possible answers.

Can the theology of baptism be made to apply to the infants of non-practising Christians?

When we considered the appropriateness of baptizing infants,[2] we conceded that the direct link between faith and baptism, observable again and again in the New Testament, is necessarily absent from infant baptism. An infant cannot be said to have faith. But, we argued, though incapable of personal faith, an infant may be surrounded by the faith of his parents and of the Church. In that faith he will be nurtured; he will be presented with opportunities to make his own response of faith. In due course, if the response is forthcoming, he will be able to ratify what was done for him in baptism by presenting himself voluntarily for confirmation. In the meantime, the faith is not his, but that of his parents and of the

[1] Jeremias, op. cit., p.87
[2] See above, pp.51–56, 65f

Church. Similarly, the child who is born into a Christian family may be said to belong to *the* Christian Family, not because he has voluntarily identified himself with it, but because he has been born into it. As an infant he can no more choose the Family to which he belongs than he can choose his parents. Later on, of course, he can repudiate the Church, as indeed he could repudiate his human family. But that is immaterial. The possibility that he may subsequently lapse does not affect the validity of his baptism. The child is born into the divine Family.

How do these understandings of the appropriateness of infant baptism fare when they are applied to infants whose parents are not practising Christians? We are bound to admit, of course, that it is impossible to judge the extent of another's faith, although the level of the parents' commitment to the Body of Christ can be estimated in an objective way. Some evangelicals would point out that it is possible even for 'church members, regular in attendance at services'[3] to be lacking in saving faith, though it is difficult to see what the Church could possibly do to surmount that problem. But if we accept the argument of Chapter Six that many parents seek their children's baptisms for reasons that have nothing at all to do with their own personal Christian faith or commitment to Christ, we cannot argue that their children can justifiably be baptized on the strength of their parents' faith.

There remains the faith of the Church. The local congregation in its life and worship represents the universal Church into which children are received by baptism. In microcosm it is the Community of Faith. Can the faith of the congregation be said to make up that which is lacking in the parents? Some writers suggest that this is in fact the case, and that the Church's faith is actually more important than that of the parents, and sometimes the parents' faith is not mentioned at all. Thus the Methodist Statement of 1952, in discussing the relationship between baptism and faith, asserts that 'the sacrament is never administered without the response of faith, the faith of the assembly of believing people', but

[3] Bridge and Phypers, op. cit., p.157

does not consider the faith of parents.[4] But it is difficult to find theological justification for emphasizing only, or even primarily, the faith of the Church. As Marcel says,

> The Church . . . can only grant baptism if at least one of the child's parents avows belief in the Lord's promise. In the perspective of the covenant the baptism of the child is truly what it claims to be only if faith is present in the family that demands it. The faith of the Church cannot make up for the absence of faith in the parents.[5]

The vicarious faith of which the New Testament speaks is always that of a person or persons close to the individual involved. This in turn raises a practical consideration, which may, in the long run, be the determining factor in deciding whether or not the Church's faith can make up for a deficiency in parental faith. For if, despite Marcel, the faith of the Church is to be the warrant for a child's baptism, then the Church must be able to envelope the child with faith during his childhood and adolescence. The local congregation must take its promises seriously and

> the minister must establish the Church's right of access to keep the promises which its members make. Where 'fringe' families are concerned and the perseverance, if not the good intentions, of the parents is in question, then more responsibility than ever falls on the congregation. Their faith and effort must make up what is lacking and it should be made clear to the parents that no effort will be spared to do so.[6]

But even so, can the Church's faith really be an adequate substitute for parental faith? Clearly it will be present at the moment of baptism and will continue to be present. But to what extent will the growing child become aware of it? He may (perhaps) attend Sunday school for one hour out of every

---

[4] Methodist Conference *Minutes*, 1952, p.228. The Statement later makes reference to the ability (or otherwise) of the parents to pledge themselves to give the promises, but this is a separate issue from that of their faith, as we subsequently argue (see below, pp.140ff.). John Stacey, op. cit., p.336, also stresses the faith of the Church, describes the promises of the parents as of secondary importance, but makes no explicit reference to the *faith* of the parents

[5] Marcel, op. cit., p.234

[6] Chave, op. cit., p.76

168; his home may occasionally be visited by the minister or one or two church members. But this can hardly be thought to be sufficient nurture in the faith.

Even greater difficulties are presented by the Christian family argument. A child is not a member of *the* Christian Family by birth into a Christian family if his parents are not committed, practising Christians. It could indeed be said that to baptize him would be to make him a member of *the* Christian Family, *despite* his human family; and there is nothing in the traditional case to justify this, unless one accepts the view that the baptism of any infant is acceptable because baptism is a declaration of the prevenient grace of God.[7] David Stacey, though not arguing for absolutely indiscriminate baptism, would contend, on these grounds, that no request from parents who are willing to make the baptismal promises should be refused:

> In baptism God gives himself to the child and also claims the child for his own. Just as the creation of physical life remains an act of sovereign love, though it cannot possibly meet with immediate, grateful response, so the initiation of spiritual life is unaffected by the inability of the child to respond. God's actions are not conditioned by our responses . . . God not merely receives, but proclaims that he receives. The baptism of infants declares that God's answer to the present evil world is the creation of a new Israel, sheltered and protected by him, in which all are welcome . . . Children are received into the New Israel because they are members of the human race and objects of God's love, and because they have not wilfully resisted him. Such a reversal of normal standards is this that one might almost say that children are more suitable for the covenant than adults. They are not weighed down with the worldly wisdom that dulls adult receptivity. God grasps more easily those who are too young to struggle. Thus infant baptism witnesses to the true nature of the gospel, to its 'objective givenness', to the fact that it is centred in the gracious activity of God . . . Several reasons for 'indiscriminate' baptism emerge. First, in receiving all children regardless of the faith of their parents we are repeating what

[7] R. R. Osborn, op. cit., presents a case for 'general' baptism based partly on the presumed Christianity of parents in a Christian country, but primarily upon the fact that baptism is a declaration of God's prevenient grace and a means of grace to the recipient

Christ himself did in his earthly life (Mark 9:36, 10:14). The grace of God is for all men, Christ died for all, and all children have, therefore, as their birth-right free admittance into the realm of grace. To refuse baptism when it is requested is to attempt to restrict the grace of God. Secondly, the sacrament preaches the evangelical gospel, and the less virtuous the parents are the less chance there is of confusion as to where the real initiative lives. This sacrament demonstrates to society with water rather than words that Christ came to save not the righteous, but the whole race.[8]

There is a great deal of force in this argument. We have seen that again and again the New Testament declares God's grace to be the prime mover in mankind's salvation. This prevenient grace precedes a believer's desire to be baptized; by the same token, it precedes a person's faith and even his capacity for faith. God's love is available to all mankind; baptism is a sign of the New Covenant; in baptizing any infant, however committed or uncommitted his parents may be, we declare that God promises that child a place in the fellowship of the covenant people.

But there are three things to be said against it. First, it quite improperly seizes upon one of the traditional justifications for infant baptism to the exclusion of certain others. It is special pleading to state that baptism is 'primarily' a sign of God's gracious love to all mankind (just as it is special pleading when the baptist maintains that baptism is 'primarily' a sign of faith already exercised). Stacey is right to emphasize the prevenience of grace, but wrong to ignore the need for the presence of faith, albeit vicarious faith. This justification for indiscriminate baptism can stand only if it is believed that it is proper to make a radical departure from the traditional understanding of infant baptism *in its fullness* by ignoring one of the New Testament's major insights into the meaning of baptism; baptism is administered in the presence of faith.

Second, as we saw in Chapter Three,[9] the logic of this

---

[8] W. David Stacey in *The London Quarterly and Holborn Review,* July 1961, pp.187f. Stacey supplies three other reasons for allowing indiscriminate baptism, all of them of a practical rather than a theological nature; see below, p.137

[9] See above, pp.51, 66f.

argument should lead to absolutely indiscriminate baptism. 'The less virtuous the parents are the less chance there is of confusion as to where the real initiative lies,' writes David Stacey. Not surprisingly, however, he stops short of the absurdity to which the logic of his argument leads:

> Difficulty arises when the insincerity of the parents is flagrant or well known and when, consequently, vows made by them in church would be a public scandal. In such a case the ill effects of proceeding on the public at large would outweigh the good effects outlined above. Refusal is, therefore, inevitable.[10]

But this contradicts what he has already said about the parents' lack of virtue being an excellent testimony to the priority of grace. If he is prepared to justify the baptism of children whose parents

> disregard the duty of public worship, show no evidence of New Testament faith, reveal a mournful ignorance of the meaning of the rite, and, as far as one can see, have no intention of carrying out its obligations,[11]

on the grounds that such baptisms declare God's gracious and unmerited love, what theological grounds can there be for refusing any child's baptism? It is possible to make out a case for the baptism of children of Christian parents only and a (rather shaky) case for totally indiscriminate baptism. Theologically, there is no tenable middle ground.

Third, Methodists, in common with members of other denominations, are required to set great store by the promises of parents. The Church does not in practice perform baptisms simply as a sign of God's love, but seeks to ensure that parents are able to give the necessary promises. Methodism directs that

> if the parents or guardians cannot pledge themselves to give the promises contained in the service of baptism, the minister may defer the baptism of the child.[12]

[10] Stacey, op. cit., p.189
[11] Ibid., p.185. See footnote 1 on p.190 which makes clear that Stacey has such parents in mind throughout his article
[12] *M.S.B.*, p.A3

The theology of baptism, then, can only be applied to the children of non-practising Christians by being robbed of some of its biblical and historical meaning, by the use of an argument which ultimately leads to absurdity, and by ignoring the plain intention of the Church which emphasizes that it is 'Christian parents' able to 'give the promises' who should present their children for baptism.

Should parents ever be turned away or antagonized?

In Chapter Seven we saw that attempts to prepare parents, by letter and interview, and to instruct them in the meaning of baptism, are often greeted with hostility or indifference. Many parents assume that they have an inalienable right to have children baptized on demand and greatly resent being subjected to any sort of pre-baptismal preparation. Their anger and resentment is understandably intensified if and when their request or demand is refused. *The Daily Mirror*[13] recently carried a story headed 'Go-to-church row stops a baptism' which described how an Anglican priest refused to baptize the child of non-practising Christians. The priest is quoted as saying 'I am fed up with people spitting out promises they don't intend to keep'; and the father is described as 'angry' about the priest's attitude. This sort of story, which the Church finds unedifying but in which the popular press delights, brings into focus two important questions: has the Church any right to antagonize people? Has a minister any right to refuse a baptism?

The fact that interviews may be regarded by some parents as an unnecessary and burdensome preliminary to baptism cannot be considered to be an argument against them. If parents are unwilling to undergo this very basic preparation, the seriousness of their desire to have their child baptized is open to question. However much some parents may be antagonized by interviews, there can be no doubt that they should take place.

But granted that interviews, though unpopular, are necessary, has the Church any right to antagonize people by refusing to baptize their children? Categorical refusals are no doubt rare, but some ministers who believe that there is no

[13] 27 June 1977

justification for baptizing any infants other than those whose parents are practising Christians are prepared, at the end of the day, to say 'no'. For the most part, however, ministers who accept the theological case for reserving baptism for the children of practising Christians would prefer to dissuade rather than to refuse:

> Certainly the promises mean more than nominal Christians can conscientiously promise, and instruction should point this out. It is often said that the best policy is that the minister makes this so clear that the parents either resume the practice of their religion or declare that they cannot conscientiously make the promises, and so withdraw their request. It is said to be a kind of proof of the thoroughness of the instruction if the latter sometimes happens.[14]

One of the ministers quoted in Chapter Seven revealed that the great majority of the recipients of his letter do not ask for an interview, thus saving him a good deal of time. Another remarked that his very moderately worded document had 'resulted in several people saying that they will not proceed further with the matter'. If written documents can produce this result, there can be little doubt that interviews can do the same, and probably more effectively. It is surely no accident that the ministers who have the most scruples about baptizing the children of non-practising Christians seem also to be the ones who find most parents withdrawing their request. The minister's handling of an interview is crucial: if he takes a rigorous line, he may well prefer the parents to withdraw rather than finding himself in the position of having to refuse their child's baptism. Consciously or sub-consciously, therefore, he will be inclined to manipulate the interview towards that end.

Should a minister rejoice when, after discussion and thought, parents are honest enough to admit that they cannot conscientiously make the promises and so do not proceed with the matter; or should he conclude that a stumbling-block has been placed quite unnecessarily in the way of one of Christ's little ones? When they have had time to reflect, may the parents not regret both their willingness to accept the minister's arguments and their withdrawal of their request?

[14] George, *E.R.,* p.62

May they not become bitter, and feel that the Church has no place for them or for their child?

Is it indeed possible that pastoral considerations should override theological convictions? We have maintained that it is necessary on theological grounds for the parents to be practising Christians; but could it not be that the positive advantages of receiving a family into the Church's sphere of influence, of accepting people as they are without making heavy demands upon them, should be deemed to outweigh the obvious pastoral disadvantages of antagonizing parents in the interests of theological soundness? May it be that baptism should be administered in order to forge a link with a family, as a result of which seeds may be sown, in child and in parents, which will bear fruit in years to come? Is this what is meant by the 'evangelical opportunity which we may not neglect'?[15]

To argue in this way, exalting pastoral benefits over theological convictions, is indefensible. David Stacey adduces three possible pastoral benefits which might derive from indiscriminate baptism,[16] but quite properly admits that these reasons for baptizing 'would not stand without the support of the theological argument'.[17] If we reject the theological argument for indiscriminate baptism, no practical consideration, however weighty, can justify the practice. In any case, as we shall argue below, many of the alleged pastoral advantages are more imaginary than real.

It follows from this that non-practising Christians must be prevented from presenting their children for baptism, whether by dissuasion or by outright refusal. The Church should never cause needless offence; nor should it be afraid to cause offence where necessary. In the matter of infant baptism, if parents are antagonized by a justifiable refusal to baptize a child, then the Church will feel regret. But it should not hesitate to take an unpopular stand in the interests of theologically justified practice.

Does a rigorous policy bear better fruit than a lax policy?

Practicalities must never be allowed precedence over

[15] Methodist Conference 'Statement on Holy Baptism', *Minutes*, 1952, p.226
[16] See below, p.135
[17] W. David Stacey, op. cit., p.189

theology, but it is surely permissible to use them as further support for a case which has a strong theological foundation. Both supporters and opponents of infant baptism are inclined to do this, and we now evaluate some of their arguments.

The 1952 statement of the Methodist Conference referred to the 'evangelical opportunity' presented to the Church by 'non-Christian parents' who bring their children for baptism. Only those who oppose paedobaptism in any circumstances would disagree with that statement. But opinion is divided as to whether it is by welcoming all without reserve (a policy which we shall call 'lax') or by being willing to deter non-practising Christian parents (a 'rigorous' policy) that the evangelical opportunity is best seized.

Three practical advantages of a lax policy are suggested by David Stacey, who has already adduced two theological arguments:

> Thirdly, presence at the sacrament can be a means of grace to the parents. They are obliged to hear, even to study the service. They are obliged to make vows that put strange words into their mouths. They are obliged to offer and receive back their child. They are obliged to see at close quarters the sacramental act. Without suggesting that there is anything magical in this service, it does seem reasonable to suggest that it may sometimes move the onlookers. Fourthly, 'indiscriminate' baptism provides a lesson for the congregation. The Church is a restless society, ill at ease while so many remain outside. It has a perpetual obligation, not to consume its energy in meetings and efforts and fellowship, but to seek the lost. Every baptism where a strange child is brought in is a reminder of our primary purpose. Fifthly, for every minister a request from strangers is an opportunity. Here is a chance to go into their home, to put forward the gospel (there can be no evasion in the conversation on either side), to bring them to church. Further, there is the absolute right and duty to return.[18]

The first suggestion, that indiscriminate baptism is capable of moving the parents does not seem to be borne out by observation. On the whole, baptism is at present administered fairly indiscriminately, yet this lax policy seems to be singularly unsuccessful in drawing families into the life of the Church; if

[18] Ibid.

it were successful, the membership of the Church would be rising rather than falling. It can indeed be argued that a lax policy actually damages the Church's standing by appearing to offer 'cheap grace':

> Anyone who takes the theology of baptism seriously will see at once how derogatory it is to the sacrament simply to use it as a device for retaining respect for the Christian religion.[19]

On this view, parents obtain what they want from the Church without being asked for any real commitment are unlikely to respect the Church or its sacraments or to take them seriously.

The second argument, that indiscriminate baptism provides a salutary reminder to the congregation that it has a missionary obligation to seek the lost, is open to similar criticism. A sacrament cannot be administered or solemn vows be undertaken in order to remind a congregation of its responsibilities. Even if such a course were acceptable, there is no evidence that the desired effect would be achieved. Churches are constantly being reminded of their missionary obligation, and are only confused when they see people with no obvious Christian commitment availing themselves of the sacraments. Are these parents the 'lost' whom the Church is commissioned to seek, or are they the 'Christian parents' of whom the baptismal service speaks? Perplexity and anxiety are intensified when a congregation sees a couple bringing their second child for baptism and thus making their first appearance in Church since the baptism of their first child.

As for the third argument, this is not strictly speaking an argument for a lax baptismal policy but for careful pre-baptismal interviewing. Stacey is surely correct in maintaining that such interviews should be conducted with absolute honesty, though we have seen in Chapter Seven that this aim is very difficult to achieve. Stacey seems in fact to favour the minister taking a rigorous line in interviews, though presumably stopping short of refusing to baptize a child if he is unhappy about the parents' ability to make the promises sincerely.

[19] Vidler, op. cit., p.6

This leads us naturally into the case for the opinion that a rigorous policy bears better fruit than a lax policy. On this view, the importance of the sacrament itself and of the promises made by the parents are emphasized by a rigorous policy. The minister, quoted in Chapter Seven, who observed that the majority of parents did not proceed as far as an interview after reading his letter also pointed out that 'three or four people have started attending church and every baptism has been meaningful'. His experience is not unique:

> Our baby daughter was about four or five weeks old when my wife and I decided to ask the Vicar of St. Matthew's to baptize her. We made an appointment with him to come round and discuss the details with us. To our surprise he asked us a few questions, such as, 'Are you Christians?'. 'Of course we are,' we replied. 'We were baptized and we believe in God. We admit we do not go to church except for weddings and funerals, etc., but when we need God's help we say a little prayer.'. . . The Vicar invited us to attend the Family Service . . . and said he would discuss the baptism with us later. Off we went to the Family Service, baby as well, whom we left with some very capable baby-minders in the vestry. After our first service we were impressed and surprised so we went again and again and again. By this time we had started to think again about what we had said to the Vicar at our first meeting, for by now we knew we were not Christians as we had thought . . . Eileen and I had a chat with the Vicar . . . The Vicar asked us 'Have you let the Lord Jesus into your hearts, your home, your work and everything you do?' He had no sooner asked us when both of us felt joy spring into our hearts . . . We both praise the Lord for giving us a daughter and also for directing us to St. Matthew's which has helped us find the Lord Jesus Christ, our Saviour.[20]

In view of the generally unsuccessful results of a lax policy in bringing non-practising Christian parents to commitment, it seems highly improbable that the writer of that testimony and his wife would have been brought to a living faith had it not been for the rigorous policy pursued by the church concerned, which requires that at least one parent presenting a child for baptism must be confirmed and a regular communicant. It would be quite erroneous, of course, to assume that a rigorous

[20] Quoted in *Thinking about Baptism*, a leaflet published by Grove Books

policy always produces such spectacular results, though Colin Buchanan's assessment of the evidence is that:

> it is not necessarily the being prepared to baptize which gives the evangelistic opportunity. The evidence suggests that it does not, but a baptismal policy does. The evangelism is more clearcut and the terms more fully understood in such a case.[21]

The theological argument against indiscriminate baptism must be the determining factor in deciding upon a policy; but the practical evidence seems, on the whole, to lend further support to the view that a rigorous policy is desirable.

Should the decision be left to the parents?

> Often the minister may suspect that the parents do not fully mean what they say, but the responsibility of taking the promises is theirs, not his.[22]

> Experience shows that those who desire baptism (who can say whether they desire it sincerely?) are ready to say almost anything in order to obtain it. Indeed there are complaints that the *Service 2* infant baptism service has so clearly spelled out the requirements that it deliberately encourages people in hypocrisy! Obviously the service cannot be whittled down to involve little or no commitment in order that it may meet an eccentric pastoral situation, but the very complaint shows how thousands will blandly assent to *anything* in order to secure the baptism. No doubt more and more are not now bringing children for baptism at all. No doubt some may be daunted from baptism when its terms are clearly expressed. But a great number will still assent to the terms outwardly in order to have their offspring baptized.[23]

Parents are admittedly at something of a disadvantage when they meet the minister for an interview. They want their child baptized and, unless they believe that they have a legal or otherwise inalienable right to avail their child of the sacrament, they look upon the minister as the person with the power to bestow or withhold baptism. On the whole, they are, not surprisingly, eager to say the right thing. General Direc-

[21] Buchanan, *Discipline*, p.21
[22] George, *E.R.*, p.62
[23] Buchanan, *Discipline*, p.21

tion 11 in *The Methodist Service Book*[24] refers to the minister's right to defer baptism if parents cannot give the promises, but very few parents, in the nature of the case, will admit that they cannot. Buchanan and George are surely right in thinking that assent is often given without much thought and with little sincerity.

Many ministers practise what Raymond George preaches, placing the responsibility firmly on the parents. If the parents are prepared to give the promises, the service may proceed. In the Church of England, the Archbishops' Commission on Christian Doctrine has recommended that

> if the parents are clear that baptism is what they are seeking, *and are prepared to make the promises,* they ought not to be refused.[25]

Superficially this approach seems to resolve many of the difficulties. A minister may *suspect* that parents are going to take the promises lightly, but he cannot *know*. Even if he knew, the responsibility would be theirs. But this is an abrogation of the minister's duty, as a representative member of the Church, to guard the Church's sacraments. How can he salve his conscience by disclaiming all responsibility and placing all the onus on parents? Let us consider the case, which is by no means uncommon, of parents presenting a second child for baptism who have neither brought the first child to Sunday school nor been seen themselves in church since the last baptism. The minister will, of course, confront them with this negligence at the interview, but if, in the end, the parents declare their willingness to give the promises a second time, is the minister to proceed? The parents will be delighted if he does; but they would have good reason to think that he is a fool. And will he not consider himself a party to an act of perjury?

Let us also consider those parents who join in discussion with zest when interviewed, making it crystal clear both that they are prepared to give the promises *and* that they intend to

[24] *M.S.B.*, p.A3
[25] *Baptism, Thanksgiving and Blessing* (cited hereafter as *B.T.B.*), a report by the Archbishops' Commission on Christian Doctrine, Church Information Office, 1971, p.10

interpret them in a way different from that in which the Church understands them, probably along the rather humanistic lines referred to in Chapter Seven.[26] Is the minister to proceed, knowing (rather than merely suspecting) that the parents' interpretation of the promises is inadequate? Should he accept *any* affirmative answers to the questions, no matter how diluted the parents' interpretation of them? Can the decision really be left entirely to the parents in cases like these?

Ministers are, or ought to be, reluctant to judge the sincerity of other people, though there are occasions, such as those we have illustrated, where there is little room for doubt. On the other hand, many ministers find it impossible to salve their consciences by transferring all the responsibility for the promises to the parents. We shall suggest in Chapter Ten that this difficulty, among others, may be resolved by requiring parents to give objective proof of their status as practising Christians before the minister agrees to administer baptism.

Problems concerned with General Directions

In Chapter Five we affirmed the appropriateness of the 1974 service which Methodism has authorized for the baptism of children of 'Christian parents'. Is that service, however, equally appropriate for the situation which prevails in many churches, where many of the parents are not practising Christians?

We have already considered the promises, observing the very real danger that parents will give affirmative answers to them without due thought or with little intention of keeping them.[27] No more needs to be said on that issue. We have also noted the use, within the service itself, of the words 'Christian parents'.[28] This expression means different things to different people,[29] though in an officially authorized service it must surely imply commitment to Christ and to his Church.[30]

Two other points now require consideration, both of which arise from the General Directions rather than the service itself. The first is General Direction 9:

[26] See above, p. 123
[27] See above, pp. 123, 138f.
[28] See above, pp. 90f.
[29] See Chapter Six, *passim*
[30] See above, pp. 90f.

A solemn obligation rests upon parents to present their children to Christ in baptism, which claims for them the benefits of his redeeming work, and signifies their admission into the visible community of his Church . . .[31]

Here there is no qualification. The obligation rests upon 'parents', all parents, not merely 'Christian parents'. Although the same Direction later makes it plain that baptism is administered on the parents' promise to bring up their children in 'the nurture and admonition of the Lord', the opening words of the sentence quoted may be considered an eloquent defence of any parents' demand for their child's baptism. If the Church says that they are under obligation to have the child baptized, why is the Church's local representative making such a fuss about it all? Raymond George is prepared to defend the wording of General Direction 9:

It is often said that the sentence about the obligation on parents ought to be re-phrased so as to say 'Christian parents'. Similar modifications are sometimes suggested in pronouncements on ethical questions. They almost suggest that Christianity itself is a kind of option which people may well decline. But, as the 1952 statement said, 'the gospel is for all men', and we believe that the obligation rests on all men to become Christians and thereafter as Christians to present their children for baptism.[32]

This comment raises a number of interesting questions, though we must concern ourselves only with those that are relevant to our present discussion. It may be that in an absolute theological sense Christianity is not a kind of option which people may well decline. In practice, however, it is treated as such now that Christendom no longer prevails, and the Church has no power to enforce the practice of religion, even if it were thought desirable to do so. It is indeed doubtful whether it is ever possible to do so: Charlemagne filled the Church with pagans who had been given the choice of being beheaded or being baptized, but no one can be compelled to be a Christian in any vital sense. Ultimately we are judged by

[31] *M.S.B.*, p.A2
[32] George, *E.R.*, pp.62f.

our response to the gospel, but the gospel is offer rather than demand. Once a person becomes a Christian, however, the notion of obligation becomes meaningful for him. But this brings us to the most interesting point in George's defence of the General Direction, the point at which he declares that 'the obligation rests upon all men *to become Christians and thereafter as Christians*[33] to present their children for baptism'. For this interpretation of the General Direction is one in which, with certain reservations about 'obligation', the present writer could happily concur. This is a matter of some moment. As it stands, General Direction 9, despite its final sentence, clearly states that all parents are under an obligation to present their children for baptism. But if, as George implies, this is to be understood as shorthand for the statement that all parents are under obligation *to become Christians and thereafter as Christians* to present their children for baptism, this General Direction does not in any way lend support to indiscriminate baptism. The inconsistency with the phrase 'Christian parents' in the service itself is removed.

General Directions 20 and 21 concern sponsors. Traditionally, Methodist services have made no provision for godparents although in practice many parents have appointed them. The very reasonable explanation of this omission is the immense importance which the Methodist rite attaches to parental responsibilities. The parents are the people who will most influence the child's early development: they are therefore the people who should make the promises. In the 1974 service, however, there is provision for sponsors to be appointed, though this is optional:

> Two sponsors may be appointed to assist the parents in carrying out their promises: one chosen by the parents, and the other, who shall normally be a member of the church in which the baptism takes place, by the minister. It is the privilege and responsibility of the sponsors to support the parents in the Christian upbringing of the children; to help them to carry out the promises and so to act as a link between the family and the larger family of the church; and regularly to pray for the children.[34]

[33] My italics
[34] *M.S.B.*, p.A5

The problems associated with sponsors are therefore not as great as some of those which we have considered in the earlier pages of this chapter. Yet the question of sponsorship does cause difficulties, as the following quotations from ministers reveal:

> Most parents who consult the minister have already decided on the names and the number of the sponsors, basing their decision on what their parents or friends have had to say. There is no real thought about the future welfare and upbringing of the child in the Christian Way; rather there is concern lest someone be upset because he has not been asked to be a sponsor. The importance of this is that sponsors make a promise within the service and are therefore assumed to be of Christian persuasion and willing to fulfil such a promise in the future.

> I adhere rigidly to the rubrics on sponsors: either we have no sponsors or we have one chosen by the parents and one by myself from the congregation. This is very widely resented. Most people still think of them as 'godparents' and see it as a reward for friends or family. The idea that it has anything to do with Christian upbringing is found very strange. An Anglican colleague of mine insists that all godparents are confirmed and regular communicants on the perfectly reasonable ground that only those who have fulfilled their own baptismal promises are in any position to undertake them for others. He finds this is equally widely resented.

These comments suggest that there are three problems here. First, most parents have selected 'godparents' before they meet the minister, quite often two male and one female for a boy and vice versa for a girl. They resent being limited to choosing only one sponsor. This is not necessarily an insuperable problem; it would be possible for the General Direction to be treated as a guide to the minimum number of sponsors, or one of the parentally appointed sponsors could make the promise on behalf of all three.

But second, and more significant, is the question of the sponsors' own Christian allegiance. If there is any justification for having sponsors, it surely depends upon their being qualified to help with the Christian upbringing of the child. Parents, however, usually choose sponsors on quite other grounds, and do not take kindly to being told that their appointees are unsuitable. Many non-practising Christians would probably have difficulty in finding a practising Christian among their relations or close friends. It seems right, however, that ministers should be gently insistent about this matter. Sponsors are not essential; anyone who is not a suitable person to make the promise should not be a sponsor.

Third, many parents also resent the appointment of a sponsor by the minister. Such an appointment is designed to forge a definite link between the family and the Church and to secure what Peter Chave has called 'the Church's right of access'.[35] But many parents are jealous of their own 'right' to appoint sponsors and do not welcome the idea of someone whom they know only slightly, if at all, serving in that capacity. If the reason for the appointment is tactfully explained to them some parents dislike the idea even more; they do not want any sort of follow-up by the Church. As long as the Church continues to baptize indiscriminately, there is no obvious solution to this problem, except to ignore General Direction 20. Some ministers insist upon the rule against considerable opposition, but there is evidence that others do not.[36]

A fourth difficulty can be added to the list. In churches where there are a great many baptisms, there will obviously be a practical problem of supplying sufficient suitable sponsors without overburdening those who are capable of fulfilling the role.

Because sponsors are optional, ministers may not feel bound to adhere too closely to the General Directions concerning sponsors if they feel them to be impracticable. But the problem of unsuitable parental appointees still arises, with all its attendant possibilities of conflict and resentment. The matter of sponsors is not in itself of major importance, but it serves to intensify the other difficulties of dealing with parents who are not practising Christians.

Enough has been written in this chapter to show why many ministers, who have to deal with the problem at first hand, discover that infant baptism creates for them a personal crisis.

[35] Chave, op. cit., p.76
[36] See above, p.120

Despite the efforts of writers such as R. R. Osborn and David Stacey to justify more or less indiscriminate baptism, many ministers feel that there is no adequate theological or pastoral justification for the baptism of children whose parents are not practising Christians and believe that they are supported in this view by the teaching of their own Church and the signal failure of indiscriminate baptism to bring parents to an awareness of the things of Christ. Yet in practice they are confronted by such parents who are willing to make the promises. If the ministers proceed with the baptism they are often plagued by guilty consciences; if they refuse, they find themselves involved in unhappy pastoral relationships, devoid of the clear support of their denomination. Such is the crisis. How is it to be overcome?

CHAPTER NINE

Possible Solutions

HAVING examined the many complex difficulties presented to the Church by its present practice of infant baptism, we must now ask whether there is any satisfactory solution to these difficulties. Three possible solutions will be discussed, two of them in this chapter and the third in Chapter Ten.

Abandonment of infant baptism in favour of believers' baptism

Is it right to continue the initiation of infants when it grows more and more uncertain whether they will stay in the Church?[1]

The case for believers' baptism is often argued in these days not only by those who hold the baptist view that paedobaptism is intrinsically wrong in all circumstances but also by some who accept the theological justification for infant baptism but are unable to reconcile themselves to the way in which infant baptism is currently practised. The argument may be summarized as follows:

1) Infant baptism can justifiably be applied only to the children of Christian parents.

2) Many, perhaps most, parents who present their children for baptism are not practising Christians.

3) If the parents are not practising Christians, their children ought not to be baptized.

4) Yet it is impossible in practice to make a hard and fast distinction between parents who are practising Christians and parents who are not:

[1] Wainwright, op. cit., p.25

There would be enormous difficulty in determining precisely what is meant by 'Christian parents'. The young parents, confirmed in their teens, who play no active part in church life but attend the Annual Carol Service; the member of the Young Wives' Group who never worships and whose husband has no involvement with the Church; the parents of Sunday school children, whose only allegiance to the Church is through these children—people of this sort, borderline cases, could not be refused the baptism of their children without causing them serious offence and risking the loss of the slender pastoral contacts that exist; but they could not be accepted without giving grounds for grievance and complaint to the patently non-Christian parents who would be refused[2]

5) If the significance and sacredness of baptism is to be safeguarded, and if we cannot reserve infant baptism for the children for whom it was intended and for them alone, there is no alternative but to abandon infant baptism completely and practise believers' baptism.

The adoption of this proposal would certainly resolve the difficulties that arise from the Church's present practice, for there would be no infant baptism to cause the difficulties. It has the practical virtue that it would probably be workable. It by-passes the unpleasant business of having to distinguish between Christian parents and others; the same rules would apply to all. No one could claim that the Church was practising favouritism. At first there would no doubt be complaints from inside and outside the Church, but these might conceivably be short-lived. When the fact that the Church no longer baptized *any* infants had sunk into the public consciousness, requests for infant baptism would gradually cease, and the Church could continue its work, unembarrassed by requests which it felt uneasy in granting or charges that it favoured some but not others. Moreover, in the unlikely event of such a course being adopted by the paedobaptist churches, the Ecumenical Movement would receive a powerful shot in the arm. Formerly paedobaptist churches would be brought infinitely closer to the churches which practise only believers' baptism. This, of course, is not an argument in favour of the proposal, for 'Unity at any price' is a dangerous creed, but

[2] Dixon, *E.R.*, p.11

similarity of practice would undoubtedly be a very happy by-product of such a change of policy if it could be justified on other grounds.

The proposal that infant baptism should be entirely abolished, is, however, very difficult to justify, for there are two serious objections to it. First, this policy would allow practicalities to override theology just as much as indiscriminate baptism does. There is certainly weakness in this syllogism: 'Infant baptism is theologically defensible for the children of practising Christians; it is impossible to make distinctions among parents; we must therefore administer baptism to all infants whose parents request it.' But this syllogism is no better: 'Infant baptism is theologically defensible only for the children of practising Christians; it is impossible to make distinctions among parents; we must therefore deny baptism to all infants.' The first syllogism fails to take account of the theological impropriety of baptizing children whose parents are not practising Christians; the second ignores the theological impropriety of refusing baptism to the children of practising Christians. In other words, we are confronting a proposal for which there is no theological justification, based in fact on an argument from expediency. Unless it can be shown that the practice of infant baptism can *never* be justified, the practice should never be totally abandoned.

The second objection, however, if sustained, will cut away the central hinge of the abolition argument on entirely practical grounds. Since the words quoted above[3] were first written, the present writer has revised his opinion about the impracticability of distinguishing between practising Christians and others. Chapter Ten will advance the thesis that a certain objective criterion can in fact be applied to parents, which makes the business of determining in practice which infants are eligible for baptism a practicable proposition. If it can be shown that it *is* possible to make such a distinction, the argument for the total abolition of infant baptism (on practical grounds) cannot stand.

[3] See above, p.147

Services of Thanksgiving and Blessing and Services of Dedication

It is sometimes urged that infant baptism should be totally abolished and replaced by believers' baptism, but that, to fill the gap left in infancy, the birth of a child could be marked by a service of dedication or of thanksgiving and blessing. This suggestion would be worthy of consideration if it were felt that infant baptism should in fact be abolished, but if one of the main arguments of the present work—that infant baptism is theologically justified for the children of Christian parents and should continue to be administered to such children—is accepted, the suggestion becomes irrelevant.

On the other hand, some service other than baptism may be appropriate for children whose parents cannot conscientiously give the baptismal promises. The case for such a service has recently been made by David Buckley:

> The most obvious advantage of using such a service is that it provides an alternative to the rigorist position of being able to help only those who have definite Christian commitment. Instead of turning many parents away (for this is what in practice 'deferring' baptism often means) we can offer them another service which expresses the Church's care for them and provides a link between family and Church which may bear fruit. If it is argued that such a service is theologically meaningless, I would suggest that it can be supported on the grounds of our Lord's exceptional care for children and in particular the incident recorded in Mark 10:13f. when Jesus blessed children who were brought to him; a passage included in our baptismal service but which in fact is not a reference to baptism or necessarily to believing parents! The justification for such a service therefore is that it attempts to express through the Body of Christ Christ's care for little children . . . The use of such a service of thanksgiving and blessing yields important benefits, chiefly the fact that it encourages both Church and parents to be honest and at the same time express a pastoral concern for families not involved in the Church.[4]

Buckley refers to a service of thanksgiving and blessing, a topic to which the Archbishops' Commission on Christian

[4] David Buckley in *Epworth Review*, September 1977, p.57

Doctrine also addressed itself in its 1971 report, *Baptism, Thanksgiving and Blessing.* It is necessary for us to clarify the point that this is not the same sort of service as infant dedication which many baptist churches use. A dedication service is as inappropriate as baptism for the children of non-practising Christians. This fact is sometimes overlooked by the opponents of indiscriminate baptism, but it is important enough to require further substantiation here.

Let us consider two services of thanksgiving and dedication, one published, the other unpublished. The first, written by John D. Searle, appeared recently in the magazine, *Worship and Preaching.*[5] The following is an extract from the declaration which follows the readings (Deuteronomy 6:4–7 and Mark 9:36f. or Mark 10:13–16):

> A. . . and B . . .wish to dedicate their child C. . . to God, here in the company of his people (*or* wish to present their child before God and this company of his people). With them we give thanks for this new life and for the enrichment he/she brings to their home. We unite our prayers with theirs that God will enable them to fulfil the responsibilities of Christian parenthood . . .[6]

The parents (who as this quotation shows are 'Christian') are then asked:

> Will you endeavour, with the help of God, so to order your home life that your child may be surrounded by Christian influence and example? Will you give your child access to the worship and teaching of the Church so that as he/she grows to maturity, he/she may have the opportunity to choose for himself/herself to serve Christ and join the company of his people?[7]

It is evident that this service is quite unsuitable for the children of parents who are not practising Christians. If the parents could not make the promises of the baptismal service, they could not make these promises. The same inappropriateness is found in the unpublished service, as three brief quotations from it will show:

[5] February 1977, pp.38f.
[6] Ibid., p.38
[7] Ibid.

May they (the parents) by their words, prayers and example lead this child aright.

O God, the Creator of all life, these parents now dedicate their child to you, so that your purposes may be fulfilled in and through him/her.

May he/she learn of Christ through the lips and lives of his/her parents.

In fact, dedication services are not intended for children whose parents are not practising Christians, but for those whose parents, being practising Christians, cannot accept the case for paedobaptism. The minister who devised the unpublished service quoted above describes the circumstances of its composition:

> A young couple in my church asked if I would conduct a dedication service for their baby—but not a baptism. The mother came from an evangelical mission-type church. The father has always been a Methodist, but of the conservative–evangelical type. Both attended and were members of my church, father being a church steward and mother leader of the Youth Fellowship. My problem was what to do in order to be loyal to the Methodist Church and yet to meet the request of a very sincere Christian couple. It seemed to me that if I was prepared to baptize the children of families with very tenuous links, I must do something for the child of my own church members and workers. I agreed to conduct a dedication service, but on a Sunday afternoon and without public announcement. I made it clear that this was not an authorized service of the Methodist Church. It seemed to satisfy the parents, but I must say that I did not feel at all happy about the procedure and am very doubtful as to whether I would conduct such a service again—unless it were authorized by Methodism.

There can be little doubt that demands for dedication services cause difficulties of this sort. Some ministers take the view that baptism is the only rite that should be administered to the children of Christian parents and consequently refuse these requests. Others, who are perhaps less confident in their paedobaptist convictions or more willing to be accommodating, accede to the requests. No dedication service is authorized by Methodism, but such services are not proscribed.

The justification for dedication services is that they meet the needs of Christian parents who do not believe in paedobaptism but who sincerely wish to dedicate themselves and their children to God. But these services are not without their drawbacks. First, they are likely to be confused with baptism. It is not easy for the average congregation to grasp the difference between baptism and dedication, especially if the latter borrows from the baptismal rite. John Searle's service, for example, includes the passage about Jesus blessing the children (Mark 10:13–16), the naming of the child, and the Aaronic blessing—all parts of the service of baptism—and closely resembles the baptismal service in its structure. The unpublished service has similar affinities with baptism. If the aim of the dedication service is to provide a rite which is *not* baptism, the greatest care ought to be taken to avoid similarities that could lead to a confusion of the two services in people's minds.

Second, it could be argued that the paedobaptist churches should maintain the integrity of their position by refusing to countenance any alternative to infant baptism for the children of practising Christians. Should the Church provide two rites relating to the children of Christians, between which parents can choose, or should it safeguard the uniqueness of baptism? It is at least arguable that if Methodism takes its own General Directions seriously, with their assertion of a 'solemn obligation' which rests upon parents to have their offspring baptized, it ought not to provide an alternative service for the children of its own members. Methodism has in fact declined to produce an authorized service of dedication, though it permits ministers to produce and use their own, if they feel this to be desirable.[8]

Whatever view is taken about this matter, it should now be clear that infant dedication, if it can be justified at all, is appropriate only for the very same infants for whom, we have argued, infant baptism is appropriate. It is of no use in the case of children whose parents are not practising Christians. It is important that we should make this point because it is sometimes suggested that dedication services are a possibility

---

[8] Other difficulties about dedication services are discussed in Bridge and Phypers, op. cit., pp. 174–9

for parents who cannot make the baptismal promises.[9] We have seen that this is not the case.

So we return to the subject of services of thanksgiving and blessing which, it is alleged, would allow the Church to provide a liturgical act for children whom it does not feel justified in baptizing. The Archbishops' Commission concluded that such services might be of value:

> If parents are not intending to bring up their children as Christians at all and do not recognize any obligations as binding on the Christian, the sacrament cannot be administered. Nevertheless, it is still asked for. Often as a mere social form; sometimes by articulate parents who have some theistic belief, but cannot accept the whole Christian faith or mouth the fairly explicit undertakings required in the service of baptism. It has been suggested that in such cases as these, the need so far as it can justifiably be met, would be met by a service in which blessing was set in the context of thanksgiving. No promises would be made, no sacrament administered. We believe that this would be doctrinally unexceptionable, *but only if* such a service safeguarded the uniqueness of baptism. Such a service would be appropriate for those whose own Christian belief is too minimal for them to be justified in making the promises required by the baptismal service itself.[10]

But what would such a service contain? The Commission was aware of twin dangers:

> Some services of blessing suggested for use . . . could by their particular ingredients, such as the giving of a name or the use of a formula of blessing, easily be mistaken by the uninstructed for baptism itself. It would clearly be doctrinally wrong, as well as pastorally inexpedient, to countenance any service that could give rise to such confusion . . . Further, there are dangers in making the service so minimal that it will have the effect of preaching a diluted and non-Christian doctrine of God; that it will be a theologically debased liturgy with a theologically degraded doctrine of God.[11]

[9] See above, pp.118f.
[10] *B.T.B.*, p. 10
[11] Ibid., p. 12

The first danger we have already discussed in relation to dedication services. The second is of great importance. The service of blessing is not baptism; it does not, therefore, signify entry into the Church. Nor is it dedication, for its *raison d'être* is to accommodate parents who are unable to dedicate themselves or their child to God. What then can a service of blessing mean?

The Archbishops' Commission proposed that the service should start from that natural sense of thanksgiving that accompanies the birth of a child, should continue with a declaration of the good purposes of God for the child, and should include suitable readings (Mark 10:13–16 is suggested, despite its associations with baptism), prayer for the child and his family, and an act of blessing:

> In this act of the Church to the child and the family, the goodwill of God to the child would receive formal expression, and the integrity both of the Church and the parents would be respected in that no obligations had been incurred as a result of promises made, and no baptism administered. These will be considerable gains in the contemporary situation.[12]

In 1977, the Liturgical Commission of the Church of England produced a service entitled 'Thanksgiving for the Birth of a Child'[13] as part of the *Series 3* initiation services. This short service, which closely follows the Doctrine Commission's recommendations, is clearly distinguished from baptism. Although it includes Matthew's account of Jesus blessing the children, it contains no promises, no profession of faith, no act of naming, and no suggestion of incorporation into the Church.

The Methodist Conference of 1976 received a report from its Faith and Order Committee on the desirability or otherwise of producing an official form of service to be used in lieu of infant baptism. Unfortunately, this report failed to distinguish between dedication services and services of thanksgiving and blessing, a distinction which we have seen to be very important. Thus the report referred to 'a form of service

[12] Ibid., p.13
[13] *Series 3*, pp.12f.

for thanksgiving and dedication of a child for use when parents either have conscientious scruples or are unwilling to make the vows of infant baptism'.[14] We have suggested above that there are two distinct cases here: that of the parents who, despite being practising Christians, do not believe in paedobaptism, and that of parents who cannot make the promises. For the former, a dedication service might be acceptable; but a service of thanksgiving and blessing might meet the needs of the latter.

The report, which was adopted by the Conference, recommended that the production of a thanksgiving and dedication service authorized by the Conference was inadvisable at the present time, on the grounds that Methodism was committed to the principle of infant baptism and that 'a service which departs from our usage would be likely to confuse the Methodist people'.[15] On the other hand, 'the pastoral needs of those who are conscientiously unable to present their children for baptism must be given due consideration'.[16] So, while declining the request for an authorized service, the report stressed that

> individual ministers have considerable liberty. They are free to draw up and conduct services of thanksgiving and dedication wherever they judge it to be advisable.[17]

There is no doubt, as the Anglican Doctrine Commission, the Methodist Faith and Order Committee and David Buckley have all pointed out, that the use of a service in lieu of infant baptism would meet a real need. It would mean that ministers were no longer obliged either to baptize against their better judgment or to turn people away. It would provide all that many parents actually require from baptism, in that 'the goodwill of God to the child would receive formal expression'.[18] And it is capable of being defended theologically. There is much to be said, therefore, for the Anglican decision to produce a service of thanksgiving, and it is perhaps to be

[14] Methodist Conference *Agenda,* 1976, p.293
[15] Ibid.
[16] Ibid.
[17] Ibid.
[18] *B.T.B.*, p.13

regretted that Methodism has failed to produce an official service. After all, an authorized service is much less likely than locally-produced services to fall into the errors of saying too much (and thereby confusing thanksgiving with baptism) or saying too little.

On the other hand, it is open to question whether a service of thanksgiving and blessing can ever happily co-exist with infant baptism. To reserve the latter for the children of practising Christians and to use the former for all other children seems to be a tidy, logical and justifiable solution to our present difficulties. But two doubts remain. First, is it not the case that, however carefully a thanksgiving service was compiled in the attempt to avoid confusion with baptism,[19] one service in which an infant is a leading participant (however passive!) will not easily be distinguished from another such service in people's minds? If the baptist argument were to gain further ground, would not the confusion be compounded by the use of dedication services? The existence of *three* services related to infants—baptism, dedication, and thanksgiving and blessing—each meaning something different to the theologian but not readily distinguishable in the minds of congregations is not an edifying prospect.

Our second doubt arises from a question which we have discussed before, whether or not the Church may ever be justified in appearing to turn people away, in saying 'no' to parents who request baptism for their children, in disappointing and angering people. We concluded then that this course, although often unpleasant, may sometimes be necessary.[20] The provision of an alternative service would seem to solve the problem; as the Archbishops' Commission pointed out, an important feature of a service of thanksgiving and blessing could be that no obligations would be incurred as a result of promises made. But is it not all being made too easy, both for parents and the Church? In offering a service of blessing in place of baptism for those parents who are not capable of making the baptismal promises, is the Church lowering its own standards? We return again to Raymond George's comment on General Direction 9: 'the obligation

[19] The *Series 3* service is a model of clarity in this respect
[20] See above, pp.132ff.

rests on all men to become Christians and thereafter as Christians to present their children for baptism.'[21] Perhaps the provision of an alternative service will prevent parents from facing up to the real issue, their own lack of Christian commitment; and perhaps it will prevent the Church from taking seriously its own commission to make disciples of all men, to seek the lost.

It may be then that, for all its initial attractiveness, Buckley's plea must finally be rejected. It may be that the Church should grasp the nettle and say, kindly but firmly, to parents who are not practising Christians words to this effect: We recognize that the children of Christian parents have a place within the Church and we proclaim this belief by baptizing them. But we are convinced that, before your request can be granted, at least one of you must be a fully committed member of the Church. We can offer you a warm welcome within our church family, opportunities to learn about the Christian Faith, and every encouragement to become practising Christians. If you grasp these opportunities, we shall be delighted to baptize your child. We cannot offer you any easy alternative, for we firmly believe that, in making this offer, we are offering you nothing less than the best. It would be wrong of us to offer you anything less.

[21] See above, pp.141f.

CHAPTER TEN

Towards a Policy

IN THIS FINAL chapter we shall attempt to draw together
various conclusions which we have reached during our discussion of initiation, to suggest a possible way forward for the
Church, and to assess its practicability. There can be little
room for doubt that a great deal of soul-searching and anxiety
has been caused to ministers and others by the unsatisfactory
nature of our prevailing practice. In these circumstances it is
necessary for the Church to clarify issues that have become
more and more confused and to give its members a definite
lead.

What conclusions have we reached so far? First, we have
noted that the basic issue, whether infant baptism is theologically justifiable in any circumstances, which has been a cause
of controversy since at least the time of Tertullian, is still
being extensively debated. But second, we have argued that
New Testament theology supports the baptism of children of
Christian parents, though it is necessary to be extremely
selective in the use of New Testament theology in order to
justify indiscriminate infant baptism. Third, we have concluded that baptism admits to the membership of the Church
and, therefore, in theory at least to participation in the eucharist, though confirmation is of value as a subsidiary
rite of strengthening and ratification. Fourth, we have
asserted that the recently authorized Methodist initiation
services express the understanding of baptism and confirmation for which we have argued. Fifth, however, we have noted
that, in our own day, the majority of parents who present their
children for baptism are not practising Christians, that the
difficulties attendant upon pre-baptismal instruction make it

undesirable to rely upon the efficacy of such instruction, and that many parents are to be suspected of taking the baptismal promises lightly. Sixth, we have maintained that there is no sound theological defence for the baptism of children whose parents are not practising Christians, even though serious pastoral difficulties can arise when requests for baptism are refused. Seventh, we have rejected the suggestion that, since it is alleged to be impossible to make distinctions among parents, infant baptism should be entirely abolished; we have argued that it is not in fact impossible to distinguish eligible parents from ineligible and that the disadvantages of pursuing such a policy are outweighed by the undesirability of depriving the children of eligible parents of baptism. Eighth, we have examined alternatives to infant baptism, mentioning two distinct possibilities, a service of dedication for children whose parents, though they are practising Christians, are not in favour of paedobaptism, and a service of thanksgiving and blessing for those whose parents might be deemed ineligible to present their children for baptism. Although noting the pastoral benefits offered by such services and the fact that Methodist ministers are not prevented from using them, we have suggested that the existence of one or even two services for infants, in addition to baptism, is likely to cause confusion and may even detract from the unique importance of baptism by presenting easier options.

Among these conclusions, two are of outstanding importance. First, infant baptism ought to be administered to the children of Christian parents; second, infant baptism ought not to be administered to other children. We must now ask two further questions. How can these conclusions be enshrined in a baptismal policy? Can such a policy be made to work?

The policy

What is needed is not a suppression of infant baptism, but a restoration of baptismal discipline.[1]

Our energies should be directed to baptizing only the children of thoroughly Christian families and making as sure as we can that

[1] Marcel, op. cit., p.235

the stage is in every way set for them to make the necessary response later.[2]

Infant baptism can be restricted to the children of thoroughly Christian families only if 'Christian parents' can be effectively defined. The present writer has previously enlarged upon the difficulties of finding satisfactory criteria for recognizing 'Christian parents' and distinguishing them from others.[3] But more recently he has been persuaded that an excellent case can be made for regarding *regular communicants* as the only people truly eligible to present their children for baptism. This is an objective criterion which, if widely applied, would make redundant those inconsequential discussions about whether or not it is possible to be a Christian without going to church. The same could, of course, be claimed for any objective criterion, however arbitrary. But as Colin Buchanan, who has recently argued with great cogency for the restriction of baptism to the children of communicants, is able to show, the criterion proposed is not at all arbitrary:

> Believers are to be distinguished from unbelievers among the parents. How is this to be done? The simple and obvious answer (for the sake of clarifying goals) is that in formal and outward terms a Christian is a communicant and *vice versa*. The parents are to be living members of the Church by communion if the children are to be newborn members of the Church by baptism. There is no other way. Not only in the New Testament is the sacrament of communion the characteristic activity of the people of God, but also the times of today demand that the Church be measured by some formal means. Communion requires persons to 'stand up and be counted'. It is a semi-public activity with specific participation. Listening to sermons does not necessarily imply commitment or even agreement. But participation in communion implies both. If baptism sets formal boundaries to the visible Church, then communion sustains and corrects them week by week. Where there is a faithful company at the Lord's Table, there is the Church. And where there is the Church, the children of its members may be and should be admitted to baptism.[4]

[2] G. W. Ashby in *Studia Liturgica*, Volume 2, 1963, p.317
[3] Dixon. *E.R.*, p.11. See above, p.147, where the relevant passage is quoted
[4] Buchanan, *Discipline*, p.17

Buchanan is surely correct in maintaining that in the New Testament participation in the eucharist is 'the characteristic activity of the people of God'. We have become more and more aware in recent years that the early Church had a rich sacramental life: the sacrament of baptism was the rite of admission to the Church; the sacrament of the eucharist was the principal act of worship of that Church, in which the Christian life was regularly sustained and renewed. So, far from being arbitrary, the suggestion that 'Christian parents' should be understood to mean communicant members of the Church takes us to the heart of the New Testament understanding of the Christian life. The Liturgical Movement has helped Methodism, in common with other churches, to discover that the eucharist is the Church's essential act. Buchanan is right to link together the two dominical sacraments: those children are to be admitted to the Church by baptism whose parents (or at least one of whose parents) are 'living members of the Church by communion'.

There are several other significant merits in Buchanan's case. First, it provides a criterion that is based on an observable fact, rather than on a theoretical status. It is sometimes argued that parents who are themselves baptized are thereby eligible to present their children for baptism; but this is to ignore the regrettable fact that a great many people renounce their baptism, if not formally then at least in practice.

A slightly better argument, which many Methodists and some Anglicans would probably find more congenial, is that confirmation or full membership of the Church should be regarded as the criterion for eligibility. As far as Methodism is concerned, this ought to amount to the same thing as communicant status, for regular communion is one of the duties of church members, and the Deed of Union requires the removal from membership of those who are persistently absent from the Lord's Supper and from meetings for Christian fellowship. In practice, however, almost every Methodist church has among its members a number of people who have lapsed to such an extent that they have severed all their links with the Church, short of resigning their membership. Clearly there is a case to be made for tightening the discipline in this respect also, and on the understanding that membership would in practice represent the level of commitment which, according to the Deed of Union, it entails, it would be perfectly legitimate to consider full membership as the criterion for eligibility in respect of presenting infants for baptism. The Church of England, however, has no similar disciplinary procedures with regard to those who are confirmed, and, as we shall argue below,[5] it is important that any baptismal policy should be capable of adoption in any paedobaptist denomination. For Anglicans, confirmation would ultimately suffer from the same disadvantages as baptism as a criterion. Regular communion as a test of eligibility is not subject to this problem. The point of reference is not something that happened five, ten, twenty, or even thirty years before, but a present commitment, visibly expressed. The significance of having been baptized or confirmed years ago will vary from person to person. For some, commitment to Christ and his Church will still be a reality; for others, sadly, it will not. Regularly to communicate is to demonstrate a living commitment. It seems better, therefore, for ecumenical reasons, to speak of communicant status rather than of confirmation as the test of eligibility, though if Methodist discipline is what it is meant to be, there will be no conflict between the two.[6]

Second, such a policy might be of considerable value in helping people who oppose paedobaptism, not on strictly theological grounds, but because of its lax administration. What Buchanan says as an Anglican can easily be translated into a Methodist context:

> Indiscriminate infant baptism loses some of the Church of England's best members. They go and become Baptists. This is not because they have necessarily rejected the principle of infant baptism when it is properly administered. It is because *they have never seen it properly administered*, and thus do not know what the basic principles are. The abuse of infant baptism is so widespread that it has become almost an esoteric theological task to set up a rationale for its proper use ... Hardly surprising then that many reject infant baptism out of hand and become Baptists. Any

[5] See below, pp.169f.

[6] The proposed criterion is, moreover, entirely compatible with the ethos of early Methodism. John Wesley urged not frequent but 'constant' communion on those who were in connexion with him. See *The Works of the Reverend John Wesley, A.M.*, Volume VII, Eleventh Edition, 1956, p.142

weighing up of 'results' must take into account the fine Christian people who are currently lost to their local parish church and flee instead (often to a considerable distance) to find a Baptist congregation where baptism apparently means something.[7]

This, of course, is a practical rather than a theological argument, as are the arguments that follow. Taken alone, these points cannot justify the policy which we are advocating. But the theological argument, that it is proper to identify as 'Christians' those who are baptized and who continue to reaffirm their place in the Church by regular participation in the eucharist, can, as we have suggested, be supported by reference to the early Church. The practical merits of reserving infant baptism for the children of parents who are 'Christians' in this sense are fringe benefits of a policy which may be justified on purely theological grounds, but they are still worthy of attention.

Third, another extremely valuable fringe benefit of the proposed policy would be that emphasis on regular eucharistic worship in connection with baptism would provide additional stimulus for the increasing importance which is now being attached to the eucharist and might encourage churches to provide more frequent celebrations of that sacrament. Moreover, regular communion as a duty of church members would be stressed; this can be and should be emphasized in other ways too, but the proposed link with baptism would undoubtedly strengthen the arm of ministers and class-leaders in dealing with members who are irregular communicants.

Fourth, as we have already noted,[8] baptism should normally be administered at a service of public worship. General Direction 12 indicates this practice, which will indeed seem natural and right to both parents and congregation if the former are regular worshippers and communicants. Fifth, baptism should normally be administered at the church to which the family belongs. If the parents are active members, there will be less demand for baptism anywhere else, though on the relatively rare occasions when such requests are made,

---

[7] Buchanan, *Discipline*, pp.15f.
[8] See above, p.93

163

there will be no difficulty in checking the parents'claim to be communicants and in assessing the appropriateness of administering baptism in a church other than the 'home' church.

Finally, in the words of Wainwright,

> a discipline which restricted infant baptism to the children of communicant parents would do much to remove the scandal of the disparity between the great numbers of baptisms administered and the small number of eucharistic Christians.[9]

Some of these practical advantages would no doubt accrue if *any* strict baptismal policy were implemented. But, as we have sought to show, the policy of restricting infant baptism to the children of communicants is not arbitrary, but consistent with the New Testament understanding of ongoing discipleship.

Nevertheless, this policy is likely to meet with opposition. We have already dealt with the argument that to have been baptized or confirmed might be a more appropriate qualification for parents than to be regular communicants.[10] But there will no doubt be other arguments, of which the following might be a sample.

First, it could be said that this or any strict baptismal policy would be

> a kind of repudiation of the post-Christian nature of our society; it might even be regarded as a retreat into a ghetto.[11]

On this view, a refusal to baptize the infants of persons other than practising Christians (whom we understand to be communicants) would be a refusal to fulfil the role of a 'folk religion'. But this objection must not be treated too seriously. If the baptism of children whose parents are not practising Christians is theologically indefensible, as we have maintained, the practice should not be continued whether its abandonment would be a retreat into a ghetto or not, There is a sense, however, in which the Church *ought* to repudiate the post-Christian nature of modern society. We ought not to be

[9] Wainwright, op. cit., p.77
[10] See above, pp.161f.
[11] George, *E.R.*, p.62

prepared to accept society's slow drift further and further away from commitment to Christ and the Church; we ought not to be content to cling on to the precarious links that still exist at any price. To *play* the role of a 'folk religion' is to *accept* that role rather than the much more significant role that properly belongs to the Church. A strict policy, such as the one which we are advocating, would allow the Church to offer, not baptism to the infants of all-comers, but a clear understanding that Christianity involves commitment. It would be a spur to evangelism, whose cause is better served by showing that the gospel can be taken seriously and ought to be taken seriously rather than by propping up a distorted and inadequate version of Christianity, a 'folk religion', by the indiscriminate administration of baptism. This is far from being a retreat into a ghetto: it is an advance in real mission. As Buchanan says,

> the reduction in baptisms not only relieves the sorely-tried con-sciences of the clergy—it also enables baptism to be baptism and the Church to be the Church. And that in turn is the key to evangelism and service, to building up the people of God in love and in truth, and in the last analysis to bringing glory to God himself.[12]

A second objection might come from those evangelicals who would be hesitant to make regular communion, or any other outward sign, the criterion for eligibility. What really matters, they might say, is inward faith. But this creates enormous difficulties. Is it possible to secure agreement about the nature of the faith that would be deemed necessary? Faith can mean as little as intellectual assent to the doctrine of God's existence or as much as personal commitment to Jesus Christ. Would ministers have to evaluate other people's faith? Apart from the fact that it is impossible to see into another man's soul, such a scheme would place a tremendous burden on ministers—a burden that a general baptismal policy is designed to remove. But if it is argued that a set of doctrinal propositions should be drawn up, to which parents would be required to assent before becoming eligible to present their

[12] Buchanan, *Discipline*, p.23

children for baptism, we may reply that such a procedure would be unacceptable to Methodists, who have never made subscription to a particular set of propositions a basis of membership and would not be likely to favour the application of such a rule in the case of baptism. In any case, if faith as the New Testament and the Church understand it means commitment to Christ, this commitment ought to be expressed in ways which are visible and practical, and supremely in the characteristic activity of the Church—participation in the eucharist. An objective test of faith is required, and there is no better test than this.

Third, it could be said that 'regular' communion is a vague expression, far too inexact to be written into an official policy. Does it mean that parents would be expected to communicate weekly? Few Methodist churches present their members with that opportunity at the moment, though many people regard weekly communion as a goal towards which Methodism should aim. Does it mean that they would be expected to communicate whenever their local church celebrated the sacrament? Does it exclude those who communicate only at the major festivals (a phenomenon which does not occur only in the Church of England)? It has to be admitted that 'regular' communion is an imprecise expression. The practice of churches varies considerably; this means that the terms must be left relatively vague. But, on closer inspection, this objection is seen to be little more than a quibble. If parents communicated less frequently than a minister wished, the pre-baptismal interview would furnish him with an opportunity to make this clear. The important difference, however, is between parents who are communicants and parents who are not; and any minister will know which are which.

A fourth objection arises from the fact that many churches contain a small number of sincere and regular worshippers who, for reasons of their own, never communicate. Would it be right to deprive such people, who in all other respects are faithful members of the Church, of their children's baptism? But this is special pleading. Participation in the eucharistic life of the Church is a duty of church members, and it is not justifiable to argue against the proposed policy by citing eccentric behaviour against it. Only if communion were deemed to be an optional extra for a Christian could this objection be sustained. In any case, as full celebrations of word and sacrament become more common and truncated versions of the eucharistic liturgy appended to full preaching services become less acceptable, so too the number of faithful worshippers who absent themselves from the Lord's table seems also to be declining. Those who still never communicate usually fail to do so because of mistaken notions about the meaning of the sacrament or their own unworthiness, which can often be overcome by sensitive pastoral counselling.

We conclude, therefore, that a policy of restricting infant baptism to the children of regular communicants is capable of theological justification; we contend, moreover, that such a policy, if adopted by the paedobaptist churches would have extremely useful practical consequences. 'If the baptism of infants is ever right . . . then it is surely right in the case of the children of parents who are in the eucharistic life of the Church.'[13]

Putting the policy into practice

If it is agreed that the baptismal policy which we have proposed is in principle desirable, the only question that remains to be answered is how the theory can be put into practice. Colin Buchanan himself faces this question in the context of his own Church of England.[14] He stresses the importance of the local parish; baptismal policy must not be the sole concern of the local minister but must be discussed and decided by the Parochial Church Council. When there is agreement, the matter can and should be raised at deanery level, and at the same time other denominations in the area should be invited to consider the adoption of the policy. After this has been achieved, the matter can go to the diocese, which, after remitting it to all its deaneries, could send it on to the General Synod. Similarly General Synod would refer the issue to every diocese before formulating a national policy. It is not difficult to translate Buchanan's proposed method of procedure into a Methodist setting.

[13] Wainwright, op. cit., p.77
[14] Buchanan, *Discipline*, pp.18–23

First, we must consider the local church. Buchanan is surely right to urge that policy decisions should be reached by Church Councils, not simply by local ministers. Too often in practice ministers have attempted to solve the problem alone, possibly because they have suspected their laypeople of being incapable of understanding the issues or unsympathetic towards any change in policy. But there is evidence that the subject of infant baptism is of considerable interest to many church members. In addition to those who reject paedobaptism on doctrinal grounds there are others who are alarmed by the presentation of children whose parents' first and only appearance in church is for a baptism. This obtains particularly in churches where baptisms are frequent. The relatively recent custom of normally or invariably administering baptism at a service of public worship has brought the issues much more to the fore. When baptisms took place after morning worship when most of the congregation had gone home, or at private ceremonies on Sunday afternoons in the complete absence of the worshipping community, members of a local church were often unaware of what was happening or able to ignore the matter, in a way that is no longer possible. Even in churches where baptisms are less frequent there is a need for the issue to be discussed. After all, the congregation is expected to make a promise in the service of baptism and, to do this responsibly, it needs to know what is involved. Ministers should, therefore, discuss the subject with as many of their members as possible, and should certainly raise it at Church Council level.

There is also a very practical reason for such consultations:

> If local residents can ask for baptism, and find senior members of the local church unable to defend or explain the church's policy, then the policy is doomed. To restrict baptism to the qualified is only possible where the church has a common mind, and is able to communicate it readily.[15]

The new Methodist structures provide ample opportunity for a thorough discussion of baptismal policy; the Church Family Committee, the Consultation on Worship, the Neighbour-

[15] Ibid., p.22

hood Committee and the General Church Meeting could all be thought to be suitable meetings in which to consider the matter before a decision is reached by the Church Council. In practice, discussion will normally be initiated by the minister, who will be the person most aware of the difficulties and the basic issues, though if the minister is complacent about the problem, the matter could be raised by another council or committee member.

If agreement is reached, the local church can institute its policy. Ministers will be greatly helped in dealing with requests for baptism if they are acting not merely on their own behalf but with the consent of the local church, and, as we have seen, the policy will be capable of proper implementation only if that consent is forthcoming. Agreement within the local church is vital. But it is by no means sufficient. Agreement needs also to be reached within a clearly defined area, however small. To this end, Methodist churches will need to discuss the matter at two levels at this stage—with other paedobaptist denominations in the area and with other churches of their own circuit.

Both are important, though their relative importance will vary from place to place. In a small and relatively self-contained community, where each denomination has only one place of worship and where, from a Methodist point of view, local ecumenical links are more significant than circuit links, it will obviously be ecumenical agreement which counts for more. In a larger town, where there are several churches of each denomination, it will probably be more important, in the first instance, to seek agreement within the Methodist circuit. In either case, however, it would be desirable to secure a united policy at both levels. One of the scandals of the baptismal controversy in recent years has been that, within the same locality, parents whose request has been refused by one denomination have been able to get what they wanted from another denomination. This fact shows how necessary it is for local ecumenical agreement to be reached. It would, of course, be equally scandalous if one Methodist church were to impose a strict policy, only to discover that parents were able to go to another Methodist church within the same circuit which was willing to accept them on easier terms. Circuit agreement should also be considered necessary.

A Church Council which has decided to implement a baptismal policy must also determine how wider agreement is to be sought. Should the minister discuss the subject with his circuit ministerial colleagues and invite them to raise it within their own churches? Should the Church Council refer the matter direct to the Circuit Meeting? Should local agreement be sought by means of consultation between the minister and his counterparts in other denominations? Or should the matter be raised at a meeting of the local Council of Churches? In what order, if more than one approach is to be made, should the consultations be tackled? These are the sort of questions which Church Councils would need to consider. There is no one answer which can be applied everywhere; each church must determine what would be the best method of inviting other churches within its own area to join it in implementing the new policy.

Let us assume then that as a result of all the discussions instigated by a local church, unanimity is secured within a whole town, either among Methodist churches only or, better, among all paedobaptist churches. A workable baptismal policy will then be in operation. But it would be wrong to let the matter rest there. Methodists could try to take it further by sending resolutions to the District Synod or to the Conference or to both, while, at the same time, Anglicans were referring the matter to their dioceses and to General Synod, and other denominations were doing equivalent referrals. If we then assume that several local churches up and down the country were initiating discussion and sending resolutions along these lines, while simultaneously the same sort of thing was happening in other denominations, ecumenically agreed change at national level is seen to be a real possibility. If the local church were to throw a pebble into the water, it could be astonished by the extent of the ripples.

While a new national (or even international) policy, agreed by all the paedobaptist denominations is thus seen to be a possibility, the possibility is clearly remote. Years of negotiations, major advances, major setbacks, resolutions, counter-resolutions, controversy and continuing confusion would be involved. But, we would argue, if the policy of restricting infant baptism to the children of communicants is the right policy, all these years of discussion and controversy would be well spent on seeking to secure agreement to this effect. Local churches ought not, therefore, to be deterred from implementing a local policy (with as much support from nearby churches as they can muster) just because the prospect of national agreement is remote. If the pebble is not thrown into the water *somewhere*, there can be no possibility of ripples. Change can be effected only if local churches will take the problem seriously and will communicate their concern to other local churches and to the higher courts of their own denominations.

At the same time, it is important that these higher courts should, separately or together, examine the issues and discuss their findings with the districts and circuits, or their equivalents. All the paedobaptist denominations have done this to some extent in recent years, though it can hardly be said, for example, that the Methodist Conference statements have really grappled with the question of eligibility for baptism or have done much to assuage the doubts and fears which so many people have about our present practice of infant baptism.[16] In the light of the present debate, it would be extremely helpful if the higher courts of the denominations could give serious consideration to the following propositions:

1. Infant baptism is properly administered only to the children of Christian parents.

2. Christian parents are understood to be regular communicants.

[16] The last thorough survey was the Statement of 1952 which recommended that baptism should not be refused to any child whose parents requested it, but suggested that the use of the sacrament might be safeguarded by careful attention to such matters as intimation, preparation and instruction, properly regulated administration, and post-baptismal pastoral care. These recommendations have strongly influenced the General Directions in the 1974 service. But it can scarcely be doubted that circumstances have changed for the worse since 1952, and that it is still 'notorious that many parents who do not themselves attend church, seek baptism for their children, often with the most vague and erroneous ideas about its meaning, and with no intention of accepting the solemn obligations involved' (Methodist Conference *Minutes*, 1952, p.226). We have suggested in previous chapters that the situation requires a more radical solution than was suggested in 1952; certainly the time seems to be ripe for a new and thorough official statement.

If the paedobaptist denominations were to discuss these propositions at national level at the same time as local churches were sending the matter 'upwards', the possibility of change would be greatly enhanced. It is no part of the argument of this book that such a change could easily be accomplished, though we have maintained that change is not impossible. Nor do we pretend that every problem would thereby be solved, for the basic issue between the baptist and the paedobaptist churches would remain. But, we would argue, the policy which we have proposed would be theologically defensible: it would meet the criteria which justify the administration of infant baptism. And it would have the added advantage that it would regulate baptismal practice in a way that would work, for it is based on an objective criterion. There is reason to think that it might even stimulate the evangelistic and missionary work of the Church. Other policies have been proposed, none of which is without deficiencies, whether they be theological or practical or both. The restriction of infant baptism to the children of communicants is a policy capable of being defended on both counts. It is worthy of careful consideration at every level of the Church's life.